John 8:31-32

...If ye continue in my word,
then are ye my disciples indeed;
And ye shall know the truth,
and the truth shall make you free.

John 8:31-32

*...If ye continue in my word,
then are ye my disciples indeed;
And ye shall know the truth,
and the truth shall make you free.*

HOLY
BIBLE

by Rick McKnight

Christian Literature & Artwork
A BOLD TRUTH Publication

John 8:31-32

ISBN 13: 978-0-9981531-4-8

First Edition

BOLD TRUTH PUBLISHING
Christian Literature & Artwork
300 West 41st ▪ Sand Springs, Oklahoma 74067
www.BoldTruthPublishing.com
beirep@yahoo.com

Printed in the USA.

February 2017
10 9 8 7 6 5 4 3 2 1

Contents

Contents

Contents

Recommendations

To whom it may concern:

Rick McKnight's teaching and singing ministry has been a blessing to me and I am privileged to take this opportunity to introduce him to you.

The first time I met Rick was in Tulsa, Oklahoma where he was the guest singer for Brother Kenneth Hagin's annual Campmeeting. The anointing was so great upon this young man and I was impressed with his dedication to serve the Lord that I asked him to come and teach at my Bible School. He was such a blessing to us all and to the student body that 1 have asked him to return several times to share from the Word of God and also in song.

We here at New Life Bible School have learned to love and respect Rick's Ministry and I highly recommend Him as a servant of the Lord and a minister of the Gospel.

Norvel Hayes

Recommendations

August 11, 1988

To Whom It May Concern:

Rick McKnight is one of our charter RHEMA Bible Training Center graduates. Upon graduation in May 1975, Rick went forth to fulfill the call of God on his life in the field of evangelism and as a pastor.

Through the years, we have watched Rick's ministry grow and develop. He is a man of integrity, sensitive to the moving of the Spirit of God, and a gifted minister of the gospel of Christ.

Rick is also a gifted singer. His music is anointed and powerful and he has been a frequent guest singer during our annual Campmeeting in Tulsa, Oklahoma.

You will be blessed by Rick's ministry as he proclaims the uncompromised Word of God.

Sincerely in Christ,

Kenneth E. Hagin

Recommendations

Pastor Kenneth E. Hagin and I during Campmeeting at the Tulsa Convention Center. I was about to sing "Thank You" for Brother Hagin's 80th Birthday.

Mission Statement

Rick's mission and vision were simple, and still are! *Isaiah 61:1-3* pretty much tells it all and he prays this before every meeting.

> *"The Spirit of the Lord is upon me, because the Lord has anointed me to preach good tidings unto the meek; He hath sent me to bind up the broken hearted, to proclaim liberty to the captives, and the opening of the Prison to them that are bound. To proclaim the acceptable year of the Lord, and the day of vengeance of our God, and to comfort all that mourn: To appoint unto them that mourn in Zion, to give unto them beauty for ashes,the oil of joy for mourning, the garment of praise for the Spirit of heaviness; that they might be called trees of righteousness, the planting of the Lord, that He might be glorified."*

A PROCLAMATION

By the 1st PRESIDENT of the UNITED STATES OF AMERICA.

When we review the calamities which afflict so many other nations, the present condition of the United States affords much matter of consolation and satisfaction. Our exemption hitherto from foreign war, an increasing prospect of the continuance of that exception, the great degree of internal tranquillity we have enjoyed, the recent confirmation of that tranquillity by the suppression of an insurrection which so wantonly threatened it, the happy course of our public affairs in general, the unexampled prosperity of all classes of our citizens, are circumstances which peculiarly mark our situation with indications of the Divine beneficence toward us. In such a state of things it is in an especial manner our duty as a people, with devout reverence and affectionate gratitude, to acknowledge our many and great obligations to Almighty God and to implore Him to continue and confirm the blessings we experience.

Deeply penetrated with this sentiment, I, George Washington, President of the United States, do recommend to all religious societies and denominations, and to all persons whomsoever, within the United States to set apart and observe Thursday, the 19th day of February next as a day of public thanksgiving and prayer, and on that day to meet together and render their sincere and hearty thanks to the Great Ruler of Nations for the manifold and signal mercies which distinguish our lot as a nation, particularly for the possession of constitutions of government which united and by their union establish liberty with order; for the preservation of our peace, foreign and domestic; for the seasonable control which has been given to a spirit of disorder in the suppression of the late insurrection, and generally for the prosperous course of our affairs, public and private; and at the same time humbly and fervently to beseech the kind Author of these blessings graciously to prolong them to us; to imprint on our hearts a deep and solemn sense of our obligations to Him for them; to teach us rightly to estimate their immense value; to preserve us from the arrogance of prosperity, and from hazarding the advantages we enjoy by delusive pursuits; to dispose us to merit the continuance of His favors by not abusing them; by our gratitude for them, and by a correspondent conduct as citizens and men; to render this country more and more a safe and propitious asylum for the unfortunate of other countries; to extend among us true and useful knowledge; to diffuse and establish habits of sobriety, order, morality, and piety, and finally, to impart all the blessings we possess, or ask for ourselves, to the whole family of mankind.

In testimony whereof I have caused the seal of the United States of America to be affixed to these presents, and signed the same with my hand.

Done at the city of Philadelphia, the 1st day of January, 1795, and of the Independence of the United States of America the nineteenth.

By the President : GO. WASHINGTON.

EDMUND RANDOLPH, Secretary of State

One
Ambassadors

We are God's ambassadors to this lost and dying world.

> *1 Corinthians 5:17-20*
> *17 Therefore if any man be in Christ, he is a new creature: old things are passed away; behold, all things are become new.*
> *18 And all things are of God, who hath reconciled us to himself by Jesus Christ, and hath given to us the ministry of reconciliation;*
> *19 To wit, (know) that God was in Christ, reconciling the world unto himself, not imputing their trespasses unto them; and hath committed unto us the word of reconciliation.*
> *20 Now then we are AMBASSADORS for Christ, AS THOUGH GOD DID BESEECH YOU BY US: WE PRAY YOU IN CHRIST'S STEAD, be ye reconciled to God. Notice the words In Christs stead! We are speaking for Him!*

Here is the definition of an ambassador - The highest-ranking person who represents his or her own government while living in another country.

We, as born again Christians, are ambassadors, from a different Kingdom to this kingdom on earth. We are in this world, but we are not of this world.

An ambassador is an official spokesman for the country he represents.

In the natural scheme of things when an ambassador speaks, he is speaking as though the King of his kingdom was speaking. All that he speaks is backed up by the country he is sent from. **An ambassador only speaks what he is told to speak.**

Matthew 28:18
18 And Jesus came and spake unto them, saying, All power is given unto me in heaven and in earth.
19 Go ye therefore, and teach all nations, baptizing them in the name of the Father, and of the Son, and of the Holy Ghost:
20 Teaching them to observe all things whatsoever I have commanded you - and, lo, I am with you always, even unto the end of the world. Amen.

Mark 16:15-20
15 And he said unto them, Go ye into all the world, and preach the gospel (Good news) to every creature.
16 He that believeth and is baptized shall be saved; but he that believeth not shall be damned.
17 And these signs shall follow them that believe; In my name shall they cast out devils; they shall speak with new tongues;
18 They shall take up serpents; and if they drink any

deadly thing, it shall not hurt them; they shall lay hands on the sick, and they shall recover.
19 So then after the Lord had spoken unto them, he was received up into heaven, and sat on the right hand of God.
20 And they went forth, and preached everywhere, the Lord working with them, and confirming the word with signs following. Amen.

These are known as the Great Commissions we were sent to deliver to this lost and dying world.

Now I know what He meant when He spoke to me these words:

From now on when you speak to demonic forces (sickness, disease, poverty, fear, depression, demons etc.) speak as though you were Jehovah! Glory!!

John 20:21
Then said Jesus to them again, Peace be unto you: AS MY FATHER HATH SENT ME, EVEN SO SEND I YOU.

1 John 3:8b
For this purpose the Son of God was manifested, that he might destroy the works of the devil.

He also came to seek and save the lost! And to tell them of the great Father God's love for them.

John 3:16
For God so loved the world, that he gave his only be-

gotten Son, that whosoever believeth in him should not perish, but have everlasting life.

Ephesians 2:4-5
4 But God, who is rich in mercy, for his great love wherewith he loved us,
5 Even when we were dead in sins, hath quickened us together with Christ, (by grace ye are saved;)

Two

Arise!

Isaiah 60:1-2 AMP
1 ARISE [from the depression and prostration in which circumstances have kept you--rise to a new life]! Shine (be radiant with the glory of the Lord), for your light has come, and the glory of the Lord has risen upon you!
2 For behold, darkness shall cover the earth, and dense darkness [all] peoples, but the Lord shall arise upon you [O Jerusalem], and His glory shall be seen on you.

Thank God! He arose from the dead!

Let's look at what happened to Jesus from the cross to the throne!

John 19:1b
Jesus said "It is finished: and he bowed his head, and gave up the ghost."

Yes! Jesus died for all mankind. But just before He died He said, *"My God, My God, Why have you forsaken me?"*

At that moment *2 Corinthians 5:21* came to pass!

For He (God) hath made him (Jesus) to be sin for us, who knew no sin; that we might be made the righteousness of God in him.

Notice it does not say he just took our sins, it says He <u>became</u> Sin for us! Sin is the fallen nature of man which Adam got when he sold out to Satan! God does not remain in the same place as sin so He turned His back to Jesus! (This was a million times worse than the physical beating He endured, or the nail pierced hands and feet!)

He was actually made to be Sin for all mankind!! Thank you Jesus!!

When sin dies, where does it go?

His Spirit plunged to the depths of hell for 3 days and nights as spoken of in:

Matthew 12:40
For as Jonas was three days and three nights in the whale's belly; so shall the Son of man be three days and three nights in the heart of the earth.

Some would have us to believe that this was in The grave. But not so and I will prove it by the Scriptures!

Acts 2:22-32
22 Ye men of Israel, hear these words; Jesus of Nazareth, a man approved of God among you by miracles and wonders and signs, which God did by him in the midst

of you, as ye yourselves also know:
23 Him, being delivered by the determinate counsel and
foreknowledge of God, ye have taken, and by wicked
hands have crucified and slain:
24 Whom God hath raised up, having loosed the pains
of death: because it was not possible that he should be
holden of it.
25 For David speaketh concerning him, I foresaw the
Lord always before my face, for he is on my right hand,
that I should not be moved:
26 Therefore did my heart rejoice, and my tongue was
glad; moreover also my flesh shall rest in hope:
27 Because thou wilt not leave my soul in hell, neither
wilt thou suffer thine Holy One to see corruption.
28 Thou hast made known to me the ways of life; thou
shalt make me full of joy with thy countenance.
29 Men and brethren, let me freely speak unto you of the
patriarch David, that he is both dead and buried, and
his sepulchre is with us unto this day.
30 Therefore being a prophet, and knowing that God
had sworn with an oath to him, that of the fruit of his
loins, according to the flesh, he would raise up Christ to
sit on his throne;
31 He seeing this before spake of the resurrection of
Christ, that his soul was not left in hell, neither his flesh
did see corruption.
32 This Jesus hath God raised up, whereof we all are
witnesses.

(The Greek word used for *hell* here is the same word used in *Luke 16.*)

Luke 16:20-31
20 And there was a certain beggar named Lazarus, which was laid at his gate, full of sores,
21 And desiring to be fed with the crumbs which fell from the rich man's table: moreover the dogs came and licked his sores.
22 And it came to pass, that the beggar died, and was carried by the angels into Abraham's bosom: the rich man also died, and was buried;
23 And in hell he lift up his eyes, being in torments, and seeth Abraham afar off, and Lazarus in his bosom.
24 And he cried and said, "Father Abraham, have mercy on me, and send Lazarus, that he may dip the tip of his finger in water, and cool my tongue; for I am tormented in this flame".
25 But Abraham said, "Son, remember that thou in thy lifetime receivedst thy good things, and likewise Lazarus evil things: but now he is comforted, and thou art tormented.
26 And beside all this, between us and you there is a great gulf fixed: so that they which would pass from hence to you cannot; neither can they pass to us, that would come from thence.
27 Then he said, "I pray thee therefore, father, that thou wouldest send him to my father's house:
28 For I have five brethren; that he may testify unto them, lest they also come into this place of torment."
29 Abraham saith unto him, "They have Moses and the prophets; let them hear them".
30 And he said, "Nay, father Abraham: but if one went unto them from the dead, they will repent."

31 And he said unto him, "If they hear not Moses and the prophets, neither will they be persuaded, though one rose from the dead."

But on the 3rd day there came a cry from heaven and the Holy Ghost entered into the dark regions of the damned and entered into the person of Jesus, made Him righteous as though He had never been made sin, and raised Him from the dead! All hell, including Satan himself could not keep Him down there!

He arose victorious over death, hell, sickness, poverty, depression, fear, and the grave!

Now He is seated at the Right Hand of the Great Father God! (No matter how many graves the Hollywood crowd digs up and shows them on the history, or discovery channel. If they find the tomb of the real Jesus there will be no bones!!)

This is known to us as Easter.

Because He arose we can arise out of Satan's grasp to a new life in Christ!

He arose out of satan's grasp so you could arise out of his grasp!

Three

Baptism in The Holy Ghost Is It for Today?

Matthew 3:11
I indeed baptize you with water unto repentance: but He that cometh after me is mightier than I, Who's shoes I am unworthy to bear: He shall baptize you with the Holy Ghost, and with fire.

Mark 1:7-8
7 There cometh one mightier than I after me, the latchet of whose shoes I am not worthy to stoop down and unloose.
8 I indeed have baptized you with water: but He shall baptize you with the Holy Ghost!

Luke 3:16
John answered, saying unto them all, I indeed baptize you with water; but One mightier than I cometh, the latchet of whose shoes I am not worthy to unloose: He shall baptize you with the Holy Ghost and with Fire.

John 1:29-33
29 The next day John seeth Jesus coming unto him and

saith Behold the Lamb of God, which taketh away the sin of the world.
30 This is He of whom I said after me cometh a man of whom I said is preferred before me: for He was before me.
31 And I knew Him not: but that He should be made manifest to Israel, therefore am I come baptizing with water.
32 And John bare record saying, I saw the Spirit descending like a dove, and it abode upon Him.
33 And I knew Him not: but He (God) that sent me to baptize with water, the same said unto me Upon whom thou shalt see the Spirit descending, and remaining on Him, the same is Him which Baptizeth with the Holy Ghost.

The Baptism in the Holy Ghost was so significant that it is mentioned in all four gospels by John the Baptist!

Well someone might say... "Did Jesus ever mention it?"

Let's look at the book of Acts to see what Jesus said after His resurrection!

Acts 1: 4-5
4 And being assembled together with them, commanded them that they should not depart Jerusalem, but wait for the promise of the Father which ye have heard of me.
5 For John truly baptized with water; but ye shall be baptized with the Holy Ghost not many days hence.

Yes! Jesus did mention the Baptism in the Holy Ghost!

So that's all four Gospels and Jesus Himself speaks of it!

Acts 2:1-4
1 And when the day of Pentecost had fully come, they were all (120) with one accord in one place.
2 And suddenly there came a sound from heaven as a rushing mighty wind: and it filled all the house where they were sitting.
3 And there appeared to them cloven tongues like as of fire, and it sat upon each (120) of them.
4 And they were all filled... with the Holy Ghost, and began to speak with other tongues as the Spirit gave them utterance!

What a thrill to know that this was the beginning of the Church that Jesus came to establish on the Earth! *(Matthew 16:18)* All of them received the Baptism in the Holy Ghost! All of them spoke in other tongues!

What is the Purpose?

Acts 1:8
But ye shall receive power, after the Holy Ghost has come upon you: and you shall be witnesses unto Me, both in Jerusalem, and in all Judea, and in Samaria, and unto the uttermost part of the Earth.

Thank God He gives us the power wherewith we can be powerful witnesses to our world!

The world, for the most part, thinks of Christians as weaklings, just biding our time until The Rapture. (The coming of Jesus for His Church.)

If they only knew we are the force holding this thing together with the help of the Holy Ghost through our prayers, and our moral influence. We are the salt of the earth, the light of the world! You think things are falling apart now? Just wait until the Christians, and the Holy Ghost influence are taken out! Talk about darkness, and chaos! I would not want to be here!

Who is called to receive this?

Some would argue and say that this was only for the First Church. Well if this is true would someone tell me the dividing line between the first Church, and the second Church?

Jesus did not say I will build My churches! He said Church ! Jesus was smart enough to build the kind of Church He wanted! Why start out with a powerful Church and wind up with a weakling Church?

Let's search the Word of God and find out who this Baptism in the Holy Ghost belongs to!

> *Acts 2:38-39*
> *38 Repent and be baptized every one of you in the name of Jesus Christ for the remission of sins, and you shall receive the gift of the Holy Ghost!*
> *39 For the promise is unto you, and to your children,*

and to all that are afar off, even as many as the Lord our God shall call!

How many has God called?

So dear reader this would include you and everyone else that God has called! How many has God called? *Whosoever believeth in Him shall have eternal life!* This belongs to you!!

Why don't you ask the Lord to baptize you in the Holy Ghost today? And receive Power to be a witness to Jesus' death, burial, and resurrection? You will be filled with the same power that raised Jesus from the dead!

Romans 8:11
But if the Spirit of him that raised up Jesus from the dead dwell in you, he that raised up Christ from the dead shall also quicken your mortal bodies by his Spirit that dwelleth in you.

Glory to God!

Four

Become God Inside Minded

As I was in prayer a few weeks ago, I asked the Lord what I could do to become more effective for the Kingdom of God? Without hesitation He said *"Become God inside minded!"*

So needless to say I have been studying on the fact that God is in me! Most of us have been taught pretty well, if you have been in the Word of faith movement long, about we believers being in Christ, i.e.,

> *2 Corinthians 5:21*
> *"We are the righteousness of God in Christ!"*

But I do not recollect very much teaching about the fact that God Almighty is in us!

In order to appreciate this we must go back to God's original plan for mankind, while bearing in mind that He said *"I Am the Lord and I change not!"* So the original plan must still be His plan for us today! So...what was (is) the plan?

> *Genesis 1:26-27*
> *26 And God said, Let us make man in our image, af-*

ter our likeness: and let them have dominion over the fish of the sea, and over the fowl of the air, and over the cattle, and over all the earth, and over every creeping thing that creepeth upon the earth.
27 So God created man in his own image, in the image of God created he him; male and female created he them.

Genesis 1:26 TLB
Then God said, "Let us make human beings[a] in our image, to be like us.(God's original intent was to inhabit the body of man!)

When He spoke these Words to the lifeless body of Adam God's breath (Spirit) went into Adam and He became a living being! Created in God's order of being!

In Genesis 3 we find man selling out to Satan. This is referred to as "The fall of Man".

When man fell God left his body, and Satan entered in.

BUT GOD HAS A PLAN!

Now we skip over several thousand years to see God's plan for fallen man unfolding.

Jesus comes to the earth. Born of a virgin! No sin in Him! God was His Father.

Jesus lives a sinless life. Heals the sick, raises the dead. feeds the multitudes, brings hope to the hopeless!

Destroying the works of the devil!

He overcomes Satan and all his works. (Sickness, hell, death, poverty!)

He then is beaten beyond recognition, and nailed to a cross! This was fulfilling the prophecy given by *Isaiah 53.*

> *3 He is despised and rejected of men; a man of sorrows, and acquainted with grief: and we hid as it were our faces from him; he was despised, and we esteemed him not.*
> *4 Surely he hath borne our griefs, and carried our sorrows: yet we did esteem him stricken, smitten of God, and afflicted.*
> *5 But he was wounded for our transgressions, he was bruised for our iniquities: the chastisement of our peace was upon him; and with his stripes we are healed*

He gave His life for us! (All of mankind!) **He shed His Blood to cleanse us from all our sin!**

While walking with His disciples in *John 3* He gives us a flash as to why He came!

He says to a religious leader in Israel ***"You must be born again!"***

What happens to a person who gets born again?

The blood of Jesus cleanses the person from all sin! The body of that person becomes the temple of the Holy Ghost!

Can I just say it like this?

God moves back into the body of man! He is back to the original plan!

Acts 2:1-4
1 And when the day of Pentecost was fully come, they were all with one accord in one place.
2 And suddenly there came a sound from heaven as of a rushing mighty wind, and it filled all the house where they were sitting.
3 And there appeared unto them cloven tongues like as of fire, and it sat upon each of them.
4 And they were all filled with the Holy Ghost, and began to speak with other tongues, as the Spirit gave them utterance.

Whats going on? Let me say it again!

God is moving back into the body of man!

Now, if you are born again' you have more than just a religion! More than just 10 commandments! More than just rummage sales!

More than just sprinkling water, burning incense and waving smoke, and wearing robes! More than bingo!

If you have been born again you have God inside you!

1 Corinthians 6:19
19 "What? know ye not that your body is the temple of the Holy Ghost which is in you, which ye have of God,

and ye are not your own?"

(This Scripture tells me that you can have God living in you, and if you are led by your feelings, you may not be aware of it! Not taking advantage of it! Remember these were born again, Holy Ghost filled people and they were not aware of the Holy Ghost in them!!)

v 20
For ye are bought with a price: therefore glorify God in your body, and in your spirit, which are God's.

2 Corinthians 6:16
And what agreement hath the temple of God with idols? for ye are the temple of the living God; as God hath said, I will dwell in them, and walk in them; and I will be their God, and they shall be my people

Hallelujah! God is now residing in the Born again believer!

It would do you a great service to say out loud "God is in me! My body is the temple of the Holy Ghost! *Greater is He that is in me than he that is in the world*" Repeat this as you go through the day, and before you go to bed at night!

Dear friend this will make that fact real to your mind, and will create a great change in your thinking, and in your life in general!

Just see to it that you do not forget Him as you face the challenges of the day!

Five

Blood Scriptures

I Corinthians 11:23b-25
23 ...that the Lord Jesus the same night in which He was betrayed took bread;
24 and when He had given thanks, He brake it and said "Take eat: this is my body which is broken for you; this do in remembrance of me.
25 After the same manner also He took the cup when He had supped saying, this cup is the new testament in my blood, this do ye as oft as you drink it, in remembrance of me.

Matthew 26:26-28
26 And as they were eating, Jesus took the bread, and blessed it, and gave it to the disciples and said Take eat this is my body.
27 And He took the cup and gave thanks and gave it to them saying Drink ye all of it;
28 For this is my blood of the new testament, which is shed for many for the remission of sins.

Romans 3:24-25a
24 Being justified freely by His grace thru the redemption that is in Christ Jesus:

25 Whom God has set forth to be a propitiation through faith in His blood...

Ephesians 1:7
In whom I have redemption through His blood the remission of my sins, according to the riches of His grace!

1 Peter 1:18-19
18 For as much as you know that you were not redeemed with corruptible things such as silver and gold,
19 But with the precious blood of the Lamb without blemish and without spot.

1 Peter 1:2 NKJV
Elect according to the foreknowledge of God the Father thru sanctification of the spirit unto obedience and the sprinkling of the blood of Jesus Christ:
Grace unto you and peace be multiplied.

1 John 1:7 NKJV
But if we walk in the light as He is in the light we have fellowship one with another, and the blood of Jesus Christ His son cleanses us from all sin.

Romans 5:8-9
8 But God commended His love for toward us in that while we were yet sinners, Christ died for us.
9 Much more then being now justified by His blood, we shall be saved from wrath thru Him.

Ephesians 2:12-13
12 That at that time you were without Christ being aliens from the commonwealth of Israel, and strangers from the covenants of promise, having no hope, and without God in the world.
13 But now in Christ Jesus, you who sometimes were far off are made nigh by the Blood of Christ.

Colossians 1:12-14
12 Giving thanks unto the Father who has made us able to be partakers of the inheritance of the saints in light,
13 Who has delivered us from the powers of darkness and has translated us into the kingdom of His dear Son.
14 In whom we have redemption, the forgiveness of sins.

Colossians 1:20-22
20 And having made peace thru the blood of His cross, by Him to reconcile all things unto Himself
21 and you that were sometimes alienated and enemies in your mind by wicked works,
22 yet now has he reconciled in the body of his flesh thru death to present you holy and unblameable and unreprovable in His sight.

Hebrews 9:12
Neither by the blood of goats and calves, but by his own blood he entered in once into the holy place, having obtained eternal redemption for us.

Hebrews 9:22b
...without the shedding of blood there is no remission of sins

Blood Scriptures

Hebrews 13:20
Now the God of peace, that brought again from the dead our Lord Jesus that great shepherd of the sheep thru the blood of the everlasting covenant make you perfect in every good work to do His will.

Revelations 1:5-6
5 And from Jesus Christ who is the faithful witness, and
the first begotten of the dead and the prince of the kings
of the Earth, Unto Him that loved us and washed us
from our sins in His own blood.
6 and has made us kings and priests unto God and His
father to Him be Glory and dominion forever and ever.

Revelations 5:9-10
9 And they sung a new song saying thou art worthy to
take the book and to open the seals thereof; for thou
wast slain, and has redeemed us to God by thy blood
out of ever y kindred and tongue and people and nation
10 and has made us unto our God kings and priests and
we shall reign on the Earth.

Revelations 12:10-11
10 and I heard a loud voice saying in heaven Now is
come salvation, and strength, and the kingdom of our
God, and the power of His Christ for the accuser of our
brethren is cast down which accused them before our
God day and night.
11 And they overcame Him by the Blood of the lamb,
and the word of their testimony.

Revelations 19:11-16
11 and I saw heaven opened and behold a white horse, and He that sat upon him was called faithful and true and in righteousness he does judge and make war.
12 His eyes were as a flame of fire and on His head were many crowns and He had a name written that no man knew but He Himself.
13 And He was clothed with a vesture dipped in blood and His Name is called The Word Of God.
14 And the armies which were in heaven followed Him upon white horses, clothed in fine linen white and clean,
15 and out of His mouth goeth a sharp sword, that with it He should smite the nations, and He shall rule them with a rod of iron, and He treadeth the winepress of the fierceness and wrath of Almighty God,
16 And He had on His vesture and on His thigh a name written KING OF KINGS AND LORD OF LORDS!!

Six

Born Again?

John 3: 3 **You must be born again!**

Jesus said that! What Jesus said is true no matter what you have been taught, or who taught it to you!

How does a person get born again? This was the question asked by Nicodemus in *John 3. Romans 10:9* answers that question. *If you will confess with your mouth Jesus as Lord, and if you will believe in your heart that God raised Him from the dead you shall be saved!* (Born Again)

> *Romans 10:17*
> *Whosoever shall call upon the Name of the Lord shall be saved!* (Born Again!)

Now what happens to a person who gets born again?

> *2 Corinthians 5:17*
> *Therefore if any person be in Christ they are a new creation, old things are passed away (Your past!) behold all things become new. And all these things (that come with the new birth) are of God.*

God has no record of the born again person's past!! He said in *Isaiah 43:25 Your sins and iniquities will I remember no more!* Praise the Lord your past is gone forever! No matter what kind of person you were, how many sins you have committed, they are at the new birth, done away with!

Have you ever wished you could have a new start in life? Well the new birth is God's offer to do just that!! Or if you are already born again He gives us...

> *1 John 1:9*
> *If we will confess our sins, He is faithful and just to forgive our sins, and cleanse us from all unrighteousness!*

I know these things are true from the Bible, and I know they are true from experience!

I used to make my living singing in nightclubs in California. Needless to say this life was not conducive to a married life, let alone a good moral life! My wife and I came to the point of separation, and did separate for 8 months. I was on the verge of a complete breakdown through a combination of sorrow, grief, and guilt.

In my hopelessness I turned to the Lord Jesus Christ for help. (I had been born again several years before this but did not take the time to read my bible, or make Him my Lord as well as my Savior!)

I called upon the Lord and He heard me. I read the 51st Psalm to the Lord as if they were my own words, and I made it my prayer! Within several days my wife and I were back together and will soon (August 18th) celebrate our 49th anniversary. I thank God for His faithfulness!

I am a new creature in Christ and have been preaching the grace of God for many years now. The new birth is what Jesus came to give this lost and dying world!!

I had no intention of writing about my personal life when I began this article, so I know the Lord is talking to someone who may be in a similar situation. Please do not give up! Instead give in! Give in to the Lord and receive Him! He will hear and help if you will trust Him!

Seven

But Thou Shalt Remember the Lord Thy God!

Philippians 4:4
Rejoice in the Lord always: and again I say, Rejoice.

But how can God ask this of me?? It seems like all hell is breaking loose in my life!

I feel like crawling in bed and pulling the covers over my head! My political party is not in power, and even when they are, they seem to be as bad as the others! (I have to agree on that comment!)

Or you may say My wife (or husband) is leaving me, my kids are not living for God, I have just lost my job, my dog Old Blue just got run over, I have no food in the pantry.On and on we could go!

What am I going to do? Apply for food stamps, call President Obama, beg on the street corner? Become an organ grinder and get a monkey?

No! With a capital NOOOOO!

I do not write this with any animosity towards anyone, but in sincerity, and in hope that it will help!

What can I do??

> *Deuteronomy 8:18*
> *But thou shalt remember the LORD thy God: for it is he that giveth thee power to get wealth, that he may establish his covenant which he sware unto thy fathers, as it is this day.*

Normally when this passage is written or spoken about, the latter part is our focus! And that is a terrific Word alright!

But for the most part I want our focus to be on the first line! *But thou shalt remember the LORD thy God.*

In the first place it does not matter which political party is in the majority, without a return, and an Awakening to our Almighty God, it will make very little difference! A promise is easy to make, whether ever intended to be fulfilled or not, as we have all seen lately! Let me say here that I am very right wing conservative Christian man, but even the tea party will mess it up if they don't stick to their godly principles!

Now about the other problems you may be facing! Don't forget your God! Some of these problems mentioned above are serious problems!

When you are facing the most stressful, and difficult problems they were basically sent to make you forget about God, and His Word!

What will you do? Turn it over to God or try to fix it yourself! The worst thing you can do is forget about God!

Don't forget where He has brought you from, or what He's brought you through!

Make a list of answered prayers and the many things you have been blessed with!

He can do it again!

Let us look at a few for instances in the Bible!

> *Habakkuk 3:17-18*
> *17 Although the fig tree shall not blossom, neither shall fruit be in the vines; the labour of the olive shall fail, and the fields shall yield no meat; the flock shall be cut off from the fold, and there shall be no herd in the stalls:*
> *18 Yet I will rejoice in the LORD, I will joy in the God of my salvation.*

This person is in trouble!

What is his/her reaction?

He remembers the Lord His God!

He/she begins to rejoice even though it seems his world is falling apart!

Now! Let me say right here that it takes faith, and courage in God to rejoice in these circumstance! You can only get faith and courage like that from God's written Word! What brings this joy in the time of stress? **God cannot lie!!**

> *Hebrews 13:5-6*
> *5 Let your conversation be without covetousness; and be content with such things as ye have: for he hath said, I will never leave thee, nor forsake thee.*
> *6 So that we may boldly say, The Lord is my helper, and I will not fear what man shall do unto me.*

May I say right here..Yes! Be content with such things as you have, but it's alright to believe God for more too! The Lord is your Helper!

You can say that boldly because He said it!

We have many such stories in God's Word!

Daniel remembered His God as he faced the lions in the den!

The three Hebrew children remembered their God as they faced the fiery furnace with courage!

David faced Goliath as he remembered His God Who had delivered him from a lion and a bear!

Remember this! All things are possible with God!

All things are possible to him that believes!!

Philippians 4:4-8
4 Rejoice in the Lord always: and again I say, Rejoice.
5 Let your moderation be known unto all men. The Lord is at hand.
6 Be careful (anxious, or worried)for nothing; but in every thing by prayer and supplication with thanksgiving let your requests be made known unto God.
7 And the peace of God, which passeth all understanding, shall keep your hearts and minds through Christ Jesus.
8 Finally, brethren, whatsoever things are true, whatsoever things are honest, whatsoever things are just, whatsoever things are pure, whatsoever things are lovely, whatsoever things are of good report; if there be any virtue, and if there be any praise, think on these things.

REMEMBER GOD!

PRAY!!

WATCH YOUR THOUGHT LIFE!

THEN REJOICE!

Obey these things and rejoice!!

Before the answer comes!

Eight

Can Two Walk Together, Except They Be Agreed?

Amos 3:3
Can two walk together, except they be agreed?

Here we are going to look at a little different aspect of our faith walk, and our definition of faith itself!

Bro. Kenneth Hagin Sr. used to say concerning our comprehending the Bible "*A mountain can be approached from many directions. It depends on which direction you approach the mountain as to your perception of it.*" Same mountain, different perspective.

Hebrews 11:6
But without faith it is impossible to please him: for he that cometh to God must believe that he is, and that he is a rewarder of them that diligently seek him.

I would like to put another perspective on this Scripture without changing the meaning.

Without setting ourselves in agreement with God, and His

Word, how can we expect to obtain the results promised?

We have built a strange "wordology" around this thing called faith! We find ourselves trying to have faith, trying to believe, without really knowing how to accomplish this Bible given task. Think of it from this aspect. Faith is simply agreeing with God, and acting on it!

I believe this will excite your faith walk into a living reality! I want us to really have a look at this word "agree"! Whole hearted agreement will bring actions! If I do not act on God's Word I really do not agree with it! If I do not act on God's Word I really have not believed it yet!

> *James 1:21-22*
> *21 Wherefore lay apart all filthiness and superfluity of naughtiness, and receive with meekness* (Be teachable) *the engrafted word, which is able to save your souls.*
> *22 But be ye doers (practicers) of the word, and not hearers only, deceiving your own selves.*

There are many "believers" who think they are really believing God's Word, but in reality they are only "mentally assenting" to it.

How can we tell if we are really believing God's Word? Let me say it again!

If we are not acting on God's written Word we really have not believed it yet!

What is the cure for our unbelief?

Simply set yourself in agreement with God's Word and begin to talk, think, and act as though every Word is absolutely true! We must admit ....He is smarter than we are!

He knows more than you! So agree with Him! It will change your life! If He says it, that settles it!

For instance --

John 3:16
For God so loved the world, that he gave his only begotten Son, that whosoever believeth in him should not perish, but have everlasting life.

That Scripture (when agreed with) along with many others (and when meditated on) will eventually put a smile on your face, and joy in your heart!

Now! Set yourself in agreement & agree with that Word! Hallelujah! It will mean so much, and eventually it will register on your mind, will and emotions!

Say it! God loves me so much He sacrificed His only Son for me!

Think of it! God loves you so much He sent His only Son to be beaten, spat upon, ridiculed, laughed at, and finally crucified, for YOU!! For all of mankind!

All that is necessary to take advantage of this salvation is whole heartedly agree with what God says!

John 3:1-7
1 There was a man of the Pharisees, named Nicodemus, a ruler of the Jews:
2 The same came to Jesus by night, and said unto him, Rabbi, we know that thou art a teacher come from God: for no man can do these miracles that thou doest, except God be with him.
3 Jesus answered and said unto him, Verily, verily, I say unto thee, Except a man be born again, he cannot see the kingdom of God.
4 Nicodemus saith unto him, How can a man be born when he is old? can he enter the second time into his mother's womb, and be born?
5 Jesus answered, Verily, verily, I say unto thee, Except a man be born of water and of the Spirit, he cannot enter into the kingdom of God.
6 That which is born of the flesh is flesh; and that which is born of the Spirit is spirit.
7 Marvel not that I said unto thee, Ye must be born again.

Don't argue about it, no matter what you know, or don't know about it! Don't make the mistake of making excuses, or presenting your denominations version. Just agree with God! No matter what you have always been taught, or believed in the past.

Then do what *Romans 10:9* says!

That if thou shalt confess with thy mouth the Lord Jesus,

and shalt believe in thine heart that God hath raised him from the dead, thou shalt be saved.

Agree with that! Do it!

Simply agree with God Who cannot lie!

> *Numbers 23:19*
> *God is not a man, that he should lie; neither the son of man, that he should repent: hath he said, and shall he not do it? or hath he spoken, and shall he not make it good?*

Do that with all of God's promises, and statements of fact!

Agree with Him!

Here's another one!

> *2 Corinthians 5:17*
> *Therefore if any man be in Christ, he is a new creature: old things are passed away; behold, all things are become new.*

Any person who agrees with God and is born again is not just a forgiven sinner! He/she is a new creation. They are also made Righteous!

> *2 Corinthians 5:21*
> *For He (God) hath made him (Jesus) to be sin for us, who knew no sin; that we might be made the righteousness of God in Him.*

I whole heartedly agree with all this! That is to be our continual confession!!

How about *1 Peter 2:24*

> *Who his own self bare our sins in his own body on the tree, that we, being dead to sins, should live unto righteousness: by whose stripes ye were healed.*

**That Scripture, when agreed with,
will get you healed!**

We could go on for hours with different Scriptures!

> *1 Peter 5:6*
> *Humble yourselves therefore under the mighty hand of God, that he may exalt you in due time:*

Make this your continual train of thought, and confession as you read and meditate on the Scriptures! I whole heartedly agree with all of this!

No matter what I feel, or circumstances say, or the doctor says, x-rays or anyone else may say.

> *Can two walk together, except they be agreed?*

Hope this helps you in your journey with God!

Nine

Disciples

John 8:32
If.......you continue in my Word... THEN you are my disciples indeed and you shall (eventually) know the truth and the Truth will set (Make) you free!

Disciple means "A disciplined one" One who takes control of his mind will and emotions and his physical body and circumstances and follows Christ in his daily walk.

Discipline means the opposite of lackadaisical, slothful, lazy, apathetic, or complacent.....

One said God blesses the diligent... but has nothing left for the lazy!

Satan's Other Weapons

These attributes I just mentioned are some of Satan's main weapons to destroy the Christian's influence and rob him of his victorious walk with Christ.

When we think of Satan's weapons we most often think of

disease, fear, depression, poverty, etc.

But these I just mentioned are more subtle, but just as deadly!

Satan's weapon of slothfulness will short circuit the power of God in your life.

"Slothfulness according to Webster's dictionary is "an aversion to work; laziness; or sluggishness."

Slothfulness is at epidemic proportions in the world and even in the Christian. It's considered normal today. Slothfulness comes gradually to the born again Cristian, it does not just jump on you and overwhelm you in your spiritual walk.

For instance I remember when we would hold revival meetings from Sunday through Sunday. The crowd would grow!

Now days it is a struggle for a lot of Christians to come on Sunday Morning! Many churches have cancelled their Sunday night meetings because of a lack of attendance!

"We have all we need" people say! We don't really need God. Reminds me of the Church in the book of Revelations. God and His Word have become a side issue to many.

Slothfulness has to be dealt with! Just like swearing, or adultery, or stealing ......?

Why aren't very many people being blessed, or healed, or getting answers to prayers? Many times slothfulness is involved.

Too lazy to get into the Word! Too lazy to pray. They want a magic touch when it comes to God's blessings.

The Real Answer

The real answer is to spend their own time in prayer and Bible study. When prayed for with no results, they want to blame the one doing the praying!

Remember when you first got saved? The zeal......but over the years gradually the believer slips into the grip of slothfulness. No Bible study time, prayer time, church attendance grows further and further apart. Hard heartedness sets in, they are not responsive to God's Word anymore. What happened to the fire?

When trouble comes they search for their Bibles, and make a half hearted confession, which brings no results. They try to use last year's faith. Even say stupid things like "I don't believe in that confession business any more!

Faith is like manna.....you've got to have a new supply everyday!

This person has crowned the flesh as King over his life.

Easy Target

The hard cold truth is this person is many times a victim of idleness, laziness, and slothfulness. An easy target for Satan. Even in the animal kingdom the predator seeks out the weak, and the feeble.

1 Peter 5:8-9
8 Be sober, be vigilant; because your adversary the devil, as a roaring lion, walketh about, seeking whom he may devour:
9 Whom resist stedfast in the faith, knowing that the same afflictions are accomplished in your brethren that are in the world.

His flesh will not allow him to spend much time (if any) in prayer, or Bible study, or witnessing his faith. There are more important things to do! Like watch TV, read the newspaper, rent a movie he should not be watching, have a little drink.

King flesh has spoken!

But one day guilt sets in and they have a desire to get back what they once had!

But something always comes up! They sit down to read and get hungry, the flesh cries out feed me, or lay me down, we can do this later, I'm sleepy, or a million other excuses!

We are talking about Discipline!

Have you ever gone on an exercise program? You're going to be the next Rocky!

Join a gym! Buy new clothes, shoes, so you will look cool. Then you go!..............

You get on the first machine, and set it for 15 minutes. 2 minutes later your flesh starts screaming "Get me out of here" King flesh has spoken!

The only way you will reap the harvest is by sticking with it! Diligence! Continue!!

"We can do this later" the flesh cries out! Money is down the drain. Statistics say 85% of the people who have gym contracts never go. That's why used (or maybe not) Gym equipment cheap!

If you will push past the pain, and struggle, and soreness, you will realize your dream!

Some one said it takes at least 6 weeks to form new habits!

Whom the Lord loves He corrects!

> *Galatians 6:7-8 AMP*
> *7 Do not be deceived and deluded and misled; God will not allow Himself to be sneered at (scorned, disdained, or mocked by mere pretensions or professions, or by His precepts being set aside.) [He inevitably deludes himself who attempts to delude God.] For whatever a man sows, that and that only is what he will reap.*
> *8 For he who sows to his own flesh (lower nature, sensuality) will from the flesh reap decay and ruin and destruction, but he who sows to the Spirit will from the Spirit reap eternal life.*

"Whoever keeps pleasing the flesh.......Keeps looking at

things that please the flesh ie... unclean things, doing unclean things, speaking unclean things... will in his flesh reap corruption. (Death)

You sow to the Spirit when you read the Word and pray, listen to Godly CD's etc.

> *Galatians 6:9*
> *And let us not lose heart and grow weary and faint in acting nobly and doing right, for in due time and at the appointed season we shall reap, if we do not loosen and relax our courage and faint.*

Faint means to quit!

You can also sow to the flesh by eating, drinking, or smoking things that are harmful.

What about real praise? Your flesh does not want to...... Make it obey the Word! Discipline it! Choose! Treat it like an unruly child! Rejoice by choice!

> *1 Corinthians 9:27 AMP*
> *But [like a boxer] I buffet my body [handle it roughly, discipline it by hardships] and subdue it, for fear that after proclaiming to others the Gospel and things pertaining to it, I myself should become unfit [not stand the test, be unapproved and rejected as a counterfeit].*

> *Galatians 5:16-17 AMP*
> *16 But I say, walk and live [habitually] in the [Holy]*

Spirit [responsive to and controlled and guided by the Spirit]; then you will certainly not gratify the cravings and desires of the flesh (of human nature without God).
17 For the desires of the flesh are opposed to the [Holy] Spirit, and the [desires of the] Spirit are opposed to the flesh (godless human nature); for these are antagonistic to each other [continually withstanding and in conflict with each other], so that you are not free but are prevented from doing what you desire to do.

We need to get back that zeal, and joy, and health!

Make up your mind to kick slothfulness out of your life once and for all! Start sowing to the Spirit, get out your old tapes or CDs, get back into prayer, make your flesh like it!!

Diligence is the antidote to slothfulness!

Read *Romans 8*

Read *Proverbs 13:4,* also *6:9-11, 20:4, 26:14, 24:30-32*

Deal with it!! Or be bound by it!

Ten

Don't You Know That's Why I Came?

God created the heavens and the Earth and all that is in the world.

He then created Adam and Eve. They were to rule and reign with God over all the earth. (See *Genesis 1:26*)

Satan, a fallen angel, lied to Eve in *Genesis chapter 3.*

<u>She took the lie as the truth</u> and disobeyed God. Adam partook of sin.

This was known as the fall.

When they sold out to the devil, the devil became 'the god' of this world.

> *2 Corinthians 4:3-4*
> *3 But if our gospel be hid, it is hid to them that are lost:*
> *4 In whom the god of this world hath blinded the minds of them which believe not, lest the light of the glorious gospel of Christ, who is the image of God, should shine unto them.*

Satan brought with him all the devilish things that belonged in his fallen kingdom. Poverty, sickness, physical death, fear, depression, heart ache, oppression, and hell, and every other foul thing you can imagine.

Jesus (the Christ, or The Anointed One, as He was known in Heaven) was sent from Heaven to the Earth.

Why was He sent?

1 John 3:8b
...For this purpose the Son of God was manifested, that he might destroy the works of the devil.

To rescue fallen mankind from the clutches of Satan, and all the awful things of his kingdom.

How did He go about doing this?

Acts 10:38 AMP
How God anointed Jesus of Nazareth with the Holy Ghost and with power: who went about doing good, and healing all that were oppressed (with sickness poverty sin depression fear, heartache, etc.) of the devil; for God was with him.

Matthew 4:23-24
23 And Jesus went about all Galilee, teaching in their synagogues, and preaching the gospel of the kingdom, and healing all manner of sickness and all manner of disease among the people.

24 And his fame went throughout all Syria: and they brought unto him all sick people that were taken with divers diseases and torments, and those which were possessed with devils, and those which were lunatick (mental problems), and those that had the palsy; and he healed them.

Mark 1:40-42
40 And there came a leper to him, beseeching him, and kneeling down to him, and saying unto him, If thou wilt, thou canst make me clean.
41 And Jesus, moved with compassion, put forth his hand, and touched him, and saith unto him, I will; be thou clean.
42 And as soon as he had spoken, immediately the leprosy departed from him, and he was cleansed.

In this Scripture you can almost hear Jesus say "Am I willing?"

Don't you know yet... this is why I came?

Luke 4:17-19
17 And there was delivered unto him the book of the prophet Esaias. And when he had opened the book, he found the place where it was written,
18 The Spirit of the Lord is upon me, because he hath anointed me to preach the gospel to the poor; he hath sent me to heal the brokenhearted, to preach deliverance to the captives, and recovering of sight to the blind, to set at liberty them that are bruised,
19 To preach the acceptable year of the Lord.

Don't You Know That's Why I Came?

Can you hear Him say, "Don't you know that's why I came?"

Matthew 11:1-5
1 And it came to pass, when Jesus had made an end of commanding his twelve disciples, he departed thence to teach and to preach in their cities.
2 Now when John had heard in the prison the works of Christ, he sent two of his disciples,
3 And said unto him, Art thou he that should come, or do we look for another?
4 Jesus answered and said unto them, Go and shew John again those things which ye do hear and see:
5 The blind receive their sight, and the lame walk, the lepers are cleansed, and the deaf hear, the dead are raised up, and the poor have the gospel preached to them.

Again listen to the Master as you can almost hear Him say: "Don't you know that's why I came!"

The next time you are tempted to beg The Lord for healing or any other problem you are confronted with remember this thought from the Master!

"Why... Don't you know that's why I came!!?"

"Never let doubt enter you mind again about My will concerning these things!" saith the Lord!

Hallelujah!!

Eleven

Facing the Storms of Life

I heard Kenneth E. Hagin say this many times as he strolled across the platform preaching God's Word: "*There's no use your thinking that you are going to just float through life on flowery beds of ease! Because the storms and tests of life come to us all!*"

Mark 4:35-41
35 And the same day, when the even was come, he saith unto them, Let us pass over unto the other side.
36 And when they had sent away the multitude, they took him even as he was in the ship. And there were also with him other little ships.
37 And there arose a great storm of wind, and the waves beat into the ship, so that it was now full.
38 And he was in the hinder part of the ship, asleep on a pillow: and they awake him, and say unto him, Master, carest thou not that we perish?
39 And he arose, and rebuked the wind, and said unto the sea, Peace, be still. And the wind ceased, and there was a great calm.
40 And he said unto them, Why are ye so fearful? How is it that ye have no faith?

41 And they feared exceedingly, and said one to another, What manner of man is this, that even the wind and the sea obey him?

In these verses of Scripture we find the disciples, and even Jesus Himself, facing a storm. The disciples face it their way, and Jesus faces it God's way!

They Forgot!

The disciples completely forgot God and His Love and His mighty power! And they forgot Who they were traveling with! They forgot all the miracles they had witnessed, and what He said about, *"...going to the other side!"*

They focused their attention on the great storm.

They were obviously depending on their own wits to get out of this potentially deadly situation!

Now! What do you do when the winds of adversity begin to blow?

Jesus was at rest!

Why?

He knew that He was dwelling in the *"secret place of the Most High!"*

"He was abiding under the shadow of The Almighty!" Safe and

secure from all alarm!

Notice what He said to the storm and to them. He said to the great storm, ***"Peace be still, and there was a great calm!"***

Then He asked them the question:

"Where is your faith?"

You could take that 2 ways! Where, as in what is your faith in? And where as in, "Why didn't you use your faith?"

"I did not say let's go halfway across the sea and drown, I said let's go over to the other side!"

They let fear have its foothold and gave place to the devil!

Ephesians 4:27
Neither give place to the devil.

When you give place to fear you are giving place to Satan.

Fear is faith in reverse! Fear is having more faith in the situation to harm you, than the power of God to help you!

I remember one particular day I was worrying about some problems I was facing. The Lord asked me what I was doing and I told Him I was worried! (As if He did not already know!)

He said, *"You are acting as if there were no God!"* Boy! That got my attention, and I got my eyes back on Him and His exceeding great and precious promises as quickly as I could! I got my Bible and kept my eyes on His Word! And everything worked out marvelously! I spoke the Word and entered into His rest!

You may be facing a "great storm" today! In your body, or finances, or your mind! Here is a word of advice! Don't let the storm keep your attention! Fix your mind and your eyes on the promises and statements of fact in His Word!

> *Proverbs 4:20-22*
> *20 My son, attend to my words; incline thine ear unto my sayings.*
> *21 Let them not depart from thine eyes; keep them in the midst of thine heart.*
> *22 For they are life unto those that find them, and health to all their flesh.* (And finances, and any other storm you face!) My comments added.

Don't forget what God has already brought you through! In Him you are an overcomer! So follow these simple instructions and overcome all the storms of life!

Twelve

God Given Authority

Genesis 1:26 NIV
Then God said, "Let us make man in our image, in our likeness, and let them rule over the fish of the sea and the birds of the air, over the livestock, over all the earth, and over all the creatures that move along the ground."

Genesis 1:26 AMP
God said, Let Us [Father, Son, and Holy Spirit] make mankind in Our image, after Our likeness, and let them have complete authority over the fish of the sea, the birds of the air, the [tame] beasts, and over all of the earth, and over everything that creeps upon the earth.

In this Bible Scripture we find God Almighty (ELOHIM) giving authority over the earth and everything on it (including Satan!) to His man Adam! Adam was to rule and reign over the earth, and take care of it! It was in his hands.

Genesis 3:1-6
1 Now the serpent was more cunning than any beast of the field which the LORD God had made. And he said to the woman, Has God indeed said, You shall not eat of

> *every tree of the garden?*
> *2 And the woman said to the serpent, We may eat the fruit of the trees of the garden;*
> *3 but of the fruit of the tree which is in the midst of the garden, God has said, You shall not eat it, nor shall you touch it, lest you die.*
> *4 Then the serpent said to the woman, You will not surely die.*
> *5 For God knows that in the day you eat of it your eyes will be opened, and you will be like God, knowing good and evil.*
> *6 So when the woman saw that the tree was good for food, that it was pleasant to the eyes, and a tree desirable to make one wise, she took of its fruit and ate. She also gave to her husband with her, and he ate.*

In these verses of Scripture we find Satan AKA Lucifer (A fallen angel) arrives on the scene. He has one thing in mind! He must destroy these creatures who God had made before they take over his domain. He lies to Eve, and calls God a liar. She then believes Satan and takes a lie as the truth. Satan is a deceiver! Deception is his game. **He knows the only chance he has against these new creatures is to get them to believe his lies more than they believe God!** Notice the first place of attack! The Word of God, or God's integrity, is called into question. Where was Adam during this encounter?

The Bible says Eve partook of the fruit God had forbidden them to eat. She turned and gave some to Adam as he stood passively by watching the whole scene unfold.

He had the God Given Authority to chase Satan out of the Garden, but he did not use it!

Adam sold out the human race to one he had absolute power over!

When he did, Satan at that point, became 'the god of this world.'

2 Corinthians 4:4
In whom the god of this world hath blinded the minds of them which believe not, lest the light of the glorious gospel of Christ, who is the image of God, should shine unto them.

Now you know why the world is filled with bad things! Sin, sickness, depression, murder, rape, pornography and all sorts of depravity is running rampant in this world of ours.

Many people in the church world, many even born again Christians, are saying while all this is going on, "Well, God is in control!"

I beg to differ with them! God controls those who submit to His control, and make Jesus their Lord.

Several thousand years went by and Jesus has come on the scene! Why has He come?

1 John 3:8
He that committeth sin is of the devil; for the devil sin-

neth from the beginning. For this purpose the Son of God was manifested, that he might destroy the works of the devil.

Luke 4:18-19
18 The Spirit of the Lord is upon me, because he hath anointed me to preach the gospel to the poor; he hath sent me to heal the brokenhearted, to preach deliverance to the captives, and recovering of sight to the blind, to set at liberty them that are bruised,
19 To preach the acceptable year of the Lord.

The reason He came was to destroy the works of the devil by helping them out of their Satan induced problems! Notice how He goes about doing this!

Luke 4:23
And Jesus went about all Galilee, teaching in their synagogues, and preaching the gospel of the kingdom, and healing all manner of sickness and all manner of disease among the people.

Another reason He came was to take back the Authority that Satan had stolen from Adam, and return it to mankind!

Through His death, burial and resurrection, He has overcome Satan and all his works! Then He gave that Authority to man!

Luke 10:19
Behold, I give unto you power to tread on serpents and

scorpions, (types of devils and demons) and over all the power of the enemy: and nothing shall by any means hurt you.

Authority over our lives has been returned to us!

Authority over Satan has been given back to us!

When a person gets born again that God given authority comes with the salvation package!

Don't make the same mistake Adam did and stand by and let Satan steal your health, your joy, your peace, your family, your finances!

You have God given authority!

USE IT!

Chase satan out of your life!

Thirteen

God is Faithful

Psalms 89:1b-2
1 ...With my mouth will I make known thy faithfulness to all generations.
2 For I have said, Mercy shall be built up for ever: thy faithfulness shalt thou establish in the very heavens.

Last month we discovered that **the whole Bible is a picture of the faithfulness of God!**

Abraham and Sarah having a child when almost a hundred years old!

David defeating Goliath with a sling shot!

Daniel in the Lion's den!

The three Hebrew children in the fiery furnace!

We could go on and on but you get the picture!

God is faithful!!

God is Faithful

We found out that it is one thing to read about God's faithfulness, and another to experience it for yourself! I have had the delight to serve the Lord in ministry for many years now, going into our 40th, and I have experienced His faithfulness for myself. So when I speak of His faithfulness it is not from someone else's experience!

A little over thirty years ago my wife Bonnie and I were told that our expected baby would not be born, that Bonnie would lose the child. We prayed to our faithful God and Bonnie wound up carrying the baby to almost 10 months! We cried out "Lord it's enough"! And we had a perfectly normal baby (maybe a little larger than usual; about 10 lbs.) God is faithful!!

Another similar thing happened to our second boy. The Doctor said the child was dead, and would be still-born. He sent us from Tulsa, Oklahoma, to Oklahoma City for many tests. Sickening tests I might add. Not sickening just to her but to me as I waited!! So after all the tests were run we came home to await the results. Of course we were praying all this time. About 2 hours after arriving home Bonnie went into labor. We rushed to the hospital. The doctor we had been seeing did not even show up. He sent his assistant as he did not like to deliver still-born babies. Within 45 minutes the assistant doctor came out of the delivery room announcing we had a perfect little boy!! Hallelujah! Thank you Jesus!

Bonnie and I went to the dentist office, actually an oral surgeon. Bonnie had an infected tooth. Bonnie went in to surgery and they administered the anesthetic. Bonnie had a bad allergic reaction to the medication. The nurse came and got me and I was horrified when I saw my beautiful wife swollen up to almost twice her normal size! Her rings were cutting into her fingers, her face was swollen up as round as a soccer ball, she could barely speak. There was a nurse there who had seen this kind of reaction one time in her entire practice. She quickly administered an antidote then brought her into a waiting room. I was praying in tongues as hard and fast as I could. Bonnie could hardly breathe.

We walked out of that office within an hour and the swelling had mostly sub-sided, and the next day she was normal in size!! God Is Faithful!!

Dear friend I want you to know in the midst of all your trials and temptations, no matter what you are facing remember this - Our God Is Faithful!

Stand on God's Word
and shout the victory in every storm!

You are bought and paid for by the Blood of Jesus!

Don't give up!!

You are a winner!

Fourteen

God is In Charge?

Dont Worry! God is in charge! or “God is in control!”

I have heard these statements from hundreds of well meaning Christians as they try to comfort others in their suffering condition. I have even heard them from the pulpit!

I want to stand up and holler “If God is in control He sure has things messed up!”

Have you read the news lately? Watched the news programs on television?

Wars and rumors of wars! Famine! 45 million abortions. Murder! Rape! Economy going down the tubes! Unemployment reaching record levels! Bank and car company, and health system take overs by the Government. (Socialism creeping in!)

And some have the audacity to think “God is in charge?”

> *Psalms 115:16*
> *16 The heaven, even the heavens, are the LORD's: but*

the earth hath he given to the children of men.

You see God, in *Genesis 1:26* put man in charge. But in Genesis 3 Adam sold out his authority to Satan.

> *2 Corinthians 4:3-4*
> *3 But if our gospel be hid, it is hid to them that are lost:*
> *4 In whom the god of this world hath blinded the minds of them which believe not, lest the light of the glorious gospel of Christ, who is the image of God, should shine unto them.*

As you can plainly see by this Scripture Satan became "the god of this world" at that point! Sin entered the world by Satan deceiving Adam and Eve. Sickness, disease, death, depression, poverty, fear, and every other diabolical thing you can think of entered with Satan and sin!

But Jesus said in *Luke 10...*

> *Luke 10:19*
> *"Behold, I give unto you(my followers) power to tread on serpents and scorpions, and over all the power of the enemy: and nothing shall by any means hurt you."*

Jesus has given to the Church power and authority over all the power(s) of the devil!

We are instructed in:

> *Ephesians 4:27*
> *Neither give place to the devil.*

God is In Charge?

James 4:7
Submit yourselves therefore to God. Resist the devil, and he will flee from you.

We are told to:
#1. Submit to God! (Believe and walk in the light of His Word)
#2. Resist the devil! (Dont allow him to have his way in your life!) Everything that is destructive that comes your way is from the devil!

Don't make the mistake of thinking that everything that comes to you is from God! Don't put up with him! Resist him by speaking "It is written" then quoting what God says about your situation! That's what Jesus did in Matthew 4! Now you do it!

#3. Satan will run from you (the believer) in stark terror! You are in charge of what goes on in your life!

Praise God! He has given us a way to escape Satan's lies, and gimmicks!

Fifteen

God is No Respecter of Persons

Acts 10:1-6
1 There was a certain man in Caesarea called Cornelius, a centurion of the band called the Italian band,
2 A devout man, and one that feared God with all his house, which gave much alms to the people, and prayed to God alway.
3 He saw in a vision evidently about the ninth hour of the day an angel of God coming in to him, and saying unto him, Cornelius.
4 And when he looked on him, he was afraid, and said, What is it, Lord? And he said unto him, Thy prayers and thine alms are come up for a memorial before God.
5 And now send men to Joppa, and call for one Simon, whose surname is Peter:
6 He lodgeth with one Simon a tanner, whose house is by the sea side: he shall tell thee what thou oughtest to do.

So Cornelius sent some folks to go find Peter and relay this message to Him.

In order to fully appreciate what is going on here, you must understand that the Jewish people were very prejudiced towards anyone not of their race.

In the mean time God is preparing Peter for this culture shock! Peter goes to the roof top and has a vision.

Peter fell into a trance and a large sheet was let down from heaven filled with animals. God said ***"Take and eat."***

Peter said "Not so Lord. I have never eaten anything that was unclean!"

God basically said ***"Don't call anything unclean when I say it is clean!"*** God is preparing him for what happens next.

About that time a knock was heard at the door of the house Peter was staying in. It was the men from Cornelius's house. Peter went with them to Cornelius's house, and tells them of his prejudice.

> *Acts 10:28*
> *And he said unto them, Ye know how that it is an unlawful thing for a man that is a Jew to keep company, or come unto one of another nation; but God hath shewed me that I should not call any man common or unclean.*

Then after hearing the angel's instructions to Cornelius he makes this statement in:

> *Acts 10:34*
> *"Then Peter opened his mouth, and said, Of a truth I perceive that God is no respecter of persons."*

Then Peter begins to preach the Gospel, (to this Roman household) but before he can finish his sermon the Holy Ghost falls on Cornelius and his family, and they all begin speaking in tongues! Something unheard of to the Jewish Peter! (Romans receiving salvation!)

God is the original "Equal Rights" advocate!

His Book is the original equal rights manual!

Look at *John 3:16* and get a fresh perspective on this blessed Scripture!

> *John 3:16*
> *16 For God so loved the world, that he gave his only begotten Son, that whosoever believeth in him should not perish, but have everlasting life.*

Notice that no race, creed, religion, or color of man is excluded! It is for "Whosoever"! Now! Who does that include? That's right! Everyone that is born on this planet has an equal right to be saved, redeemed, born again. (These terms mean the same thing)

Or they have an equal right to have their own beliefs that contradict God's Word and go to hell. (I am being brutally frank!)

> *Romans 10:13*
> *For whosoever shall call upon the name of the Lord shall be saved.*

Mark 16:15-16
15 And he said unto them, Go ye into all the world, and preach the gospel to every creature.
16 He that believeth and is baptized shall be saved; but he that believeth not shall be damned.

Jesus, too, is being very frank!

Notice "Every Creature" has a right to hear and be saved.

God is no respecter of persons!

But just as in the Old Covenant the choice is left up to the individual.

Deuteronomy 30:19
I call heaven and earth to record this day against you, that I have set before you life and death, blessing and cursing: therefore choose life, that both thou and thy seed may live:

You have equal rights! You have a right to choose! No matter who you are! No matter what color, or gender, race! God plays no favorites.

Hebrews 11:6
But without faith it is impossible to please Him: for he that cometh to God must believe that he is, and that he is a rewarder of them that diligently seek him.

You can use your faith to receive any, and all the promises of God.

2 Corinthians 1:20
For all the promises of God in him are yea, and in him Amen, unto the glory of God by us.

Let me say it again! God makes all these promises in Christ to "Whosoever will!"

Now, our ancestors may have been persecuted, beaten, even enslaved. Maybe we are still being persecuted for the color of our skin.

McKnight is my name, some Irish in there somewhere! The Irish had a very hard time when we first came to America. Some of us were beaten, and even killed for no other reason than we were Irish!

Others (of many races) were persecuted, beaten and made slaves, but we cannot hold on to those ungodly things that happened and have any kind of success, or victory, or joy in our lives if we do. They will drag us down.

You may say "People don't like me because....I am uneducated, I am poor, I am black, I am Asian, I am white, then proceed to tell of all the sins of the past that have been perpetrated on "our" race or gender, or whatever you have been taught, or maybe have even experienced.

But all that will just lead to more prejudice, strife and loss for us!

Listen to what God says to all that accept Christ as Savior!

Galatians 3:28
There is neither Jew nor Greek, there is neither bond nor free, there is neither male nor female: for ye are all one in Christ Jesus.

God is no respecter of persons!

Anyone can be blessed in Christ Jesus!

Sixteen

God's Law of Faith

In *John 3* Jesus said to a very religious man (Nicodemus) *"You must be born again."*

What happens to a person when they are born again?

There are many things that happen! But what I want to speak to in this article is found in *Colossians 1:13. Who (God) has delivered us (born again ones) from the powers of darkness (Satan) and has translated us into the Kingdom of His dear Son (Jesus).*

We are taken out of one kingdom and put into another Kingdom! These kingdoms have different laws.

> *Romans 3:27*
> *Where is boasting then? It is excluded. By what law? Of works? Nay: but by the law of faith.*

For instance in the kingdom of darkness there is an unwritten law which says "Everybody has to be sick sometime."

But in Christ's Kingdom there is a law that says *"Jesus took our infirmities and bore our sickenesses!" (Matt. 8:17.)*

> *Romans 8:2*
> *For the law of the Spirit of life in Christ Jesus hath made me free from the law of sin and death.*

The laws in this new Kingdom negate the laws of the kingdom of darkness!! In this new Kingdom of the newborn there are new laws functioning!

The old "kingdom of darkness" laws are still around, but they no longer apply to you. If you know your rights in the new Kingdom and are willing to stand up for them.

> *James 4:7*
> *Resist the devil and he will flee (run in terror) from you.*

One of these Laws under this new Kingdom is found in *Romans 3:27 "The Law of faith."*

What is this Law of faith, and how does it work?

> *Romans 10:8-10*
> *8 The Word is nigh thee, even in thy mouth and in thy heart, that is the word of faith which we preach.*
> *9 That if you will confess with your mouth the Lord Jesus Christ, and believe in thy heart that God has raised him from the dead, you shall be saved;*
> *10 For with the heart man believes, and with the mouth confession is made unto righteousness.*

Jesus taught this lesson in Mark 11...

> *Mark 11:23*
> *For verily I say unto you that whosoever shall say unto this mountain be thou removed and be cast into the sea, and shall not doubt in his heart but shall believe that those things which he saith shall come to pass, he shall have whatsoever he saith!*

Notice these two things are mentioned when faith in God are mentioned!

The mouth must speak,
and the heart must believe!
This is the Faith of God! This is the Law of Faith!

Think of how God used this law when He created the universe! God said, and it was!!

God's Word gave substance to the things He was believing in His heart, and it was done!!

Right after this powerful lesson of how to use faith God said *"Let Us create man in Our image, after Our likeness, and let them have dominion (Gen. 1:26)* The Living Bible translation said *"Let's make someone like ourselves"* God intended for man to operate like Him! And He believed in His heart, and spoke with His mouth and He had what He said!!

This is the Law of Faith!!

Jesus commanded us to have the God kind of faith in *Mark 11:22. Have Faith in God* (or the margin of the Bible says *"Have the faith of God."*)

Then in *Mark 11:23* He tells us how that kind of faith operates! Hallelujah!

> *Mark 11:23*
> *For verily I say unto you, That whosoever shall say unto this mountain, (Problem or circumstance or sickness) Be thou removed, and be thou cast into the sea; and shall not doubt in his heart, but shall believe that those things which he saith shall come to pass; he shall have whatsoever he saith.*

> *Proverbs 18:21*
> *Death and life are in the power of the tongue: and they that love it shall eat the fruit thereof.*

It tells us death and life are in the power of the tongue.

Now if the Bible is true (and it is!!) then the words we speak will create our world. Good or Bad! When we speak words of fear and doubt, sickness, poverty, etc. that is what we will have.

Scientists will verify that you can change a person by the words you speak to them! If you tell a child he is worthless long enough you can actually change his personality. Then again if you tell the same child that he is loved and that he can be anything he desires (that is good things!!) you will be equipping him for success! If you are continually speaking of how you are always sick, or broke, how you can't do something, if the Bible is true, these things will come your way! Satan will see to it!

> *1 Peter 5:8*
> *Be sober be vigilant because your adversary the devil, as a roaring lion walks about seeking whom he may devour.*

How do you think he finds the people he can devour? He listens to them talk!!

How did Jesus overcome the devil? With words! God's Words! Speaking God's Words kept Him safe from Satan's attacks!! He simply said, *"It is written!"* Jesus is our example of how to live life and to operate under the Laws of the Spirit of Life!!

So my dear friend we must watch what we believe, and watch what we say! Make a decision that you are going to find out what God says and Repeat after Him! Always speak positive things and you can't get any more positive than God's Word!! Find out what God says about your situation (sickness, poverty, grief, fear) then begin to say what He says! Even if you find it difficult to believe at first keep on saying it till your heart starts believing!

Then you will be operating in...

the God kind of Faith!!

Seventeen

God Wants to Help You!

(This is a very simple letter this month. The Lord impressed me that someone needs to hear it!)

Matthew 14:25-32
25 And in the fourth watch of the night Jesus went unto them, walking on the sea.
26 And when the disciples saw him walking on the sea, they were troubled, saying, It is a spirit; and they cried out for fear.
27 But straightway Jesus spake unto them, saying, Be of good cheer; it is I; be not afraid.
28 And Peter answered him and said, Lord, if it be thou, bid me come unto thee on the water.
29 And he said, Come. And when Peter was come down out of the ship, he walked on the water, to go to Jesus.
30 But when he saw the wind boisterous, he was afraid; and beginning to sink, he cried, saying, Lord, save (Help) me.
31 And immediately Jesus stretched forth his hand, and caught him, and said unto him, O thou of little faith, wherefore didst thou doubt?
32 And when they were come into the ship, the wind ceased.

Here we find one of the shortest prayers in the Bible! A prayer made under duress! The Bible even tells us that fear was involved. Talk about stressful situations!

But I want you to notice that Jesus heard and answered Peter's prayer!

Somebody once said that Scared prayers dont work! Well if that were true Peter would have been in a sea of trouble! And we would not have the books of 1st and 2nd Peter in the Bible!

God wants to help people.

That's one of the reasons Jesus came!

He says in *Isaiah 41:10*

> *Fear not for I am with you! Be not dismayed (Discouraged) for I am your God. I will strengthen you yes! I will help you, yes! I will uphold you with the right hand of my righteousness!*

I have written in the flyleaf of my Bible concerning this Scripture...

This is God's lifetime guarantee to me!

If you want to know the truth about it the whole Bible and every promise and fact in it is God's lifetime guarantee to all of His people!

When you know Who God is, His love and His mighty

power, and His eagerness to help you, it will give you courage to go on.

No matter what the problem, or circumstance you find yourself in, simply ask God to help you! You don't have to pray and beg for two weeks.

I must add that in many situations you will have to do your part! If you need money a good place to start is to have a job! If you need healing, you must stop any activity that brings sickness to you!

For instance: Bad eating, or drinking, habits. No exercise. Not enough sleep! Taking illegal drugs, tobacco, worry, etc... His Word is His personal guarantee. But **you must get yourself in agreement with God's Word!**

> *Hebrews 6:13*
> *For when God made promise to Abraham, because he could swear by no greater, he sware by himself.*
>
> *Hebrews 6:18-19*
> *18 That by two immutable things, in which it was impossible for God to lie, we might have a strong consolation, who have fled for refuge to lay hold upon the hope set before us:*
> *19 Which hope we have as an anchor of the soul, both sure and steadfast. and which entereth into that within the veil;*

Hallelujah! He puts His reputation on the line when He makes a promise to you!

He says in *Deuteronomy 13:19-20*

> *19 I call heaven and earth to record this day against you, that I have set before you life and death, blessing and cursing: therefore choose life, that both thou and thy seed may live:*
>
> *20 That thou mayest love the LORD thy God, and that thou mayest obey his voice, and that thou mayest cleave unto him: for he is thy life, and the length of thy days:*

The choice is yours but He urges you to choose life.

Jesus said in *John 10:10* that He came to **give us Life in abundance.**

Yes! He will help you if you will learn to take Him at His Word, and believe Him! He is all the help you need!

Simply ask Him to help you!

You have not because you ask not!

Just believe, trust, and receive!

Eighteen

Happy New Year!

This is a common greeting that comes along right after Christmas.

Unfortunately there are many thousands (probably millions) of folks that face life as a struggle. A continuing battle in some area of their life. Some with financial struggles, others with physical pain, and mental anguish. Family problems abound. Divorce is a common thing. Kids with ADD.

Prozac, tranquillizers, and an assortment of other remedies for todays problems being taken by millions.

Worry! The new national pastime.

It seems WORRY has become the national past time.

By watching the news on television you would think all is doomed! With Global warming,(Hoax!) gasoline prices, utilities going up, war in Iraq and many other places. Tsunamis, earthquakes, crime seems to fill our every waking thought, terrorism on every hand.

People who want this God given country to fail. (People from within, and without)

The Lord Jesus in *Matthew 24* predicted most of these things. Along with the love of many growing cold. Love for God, and country, and in many cases even love for each other in marriages, and family!

It seems like a bleak time in human history if you listen to the mainstream media.

Is there any hope for the future?

Well let's have a look at what Jesus says about worry in the Bible!

He says, Don't do it!

He said, When you see these things beginning to come to pass See that you are not afraid.

Don't let your heart be troubled,
neither let it be afraid!

This sounds to me like that it is up to us to do something about the fears, and worries that try to plague us. What can we do?

> *Matthew 4:4*
> *Man shall not live by bread alone but by every word that proceeds out of the mouth of God.*

We as Christians are not to be influenced by what natural man says. We are to train ourselves to hear what God says about every situation. Listen to the daily news and get bummed out, or listen to what God says about your situation, and get encouraged!

Jesus said in *John 8:32*

> *If you continue in my Word, then are you my disciples indeed, and you shall know the truth, and the truth will make you free!*

(Free from worry, sickness, financial difficulties, family problems, and mental torment. Etc. Etc!) Glory to God in the highest!

The Lord spoke to me one day (While I was being tempted to worry) and said, "If you could see into the spiritual realm you would live a life of laughter, and rejoicing, and enjoy the good things of life, and you would never be afraid again as long as you live."

I said to Him "How can I see into the spiritual realm?

He said, My Word tells you how things really are, instead of how it seem to be!

God's Words are the windows into the spiritual world. What did He mean?

I asked Him the same question!

He said, "For instance have you read in My Word how My angels encamp around those who reverence Me?"

I said, "Yes."

"Well if you could see into the spiritual realm, He said, "You would see yourself, and others who trust in Me, surrounded by My mighty angels. They are there primarily to see to it that you are protected."

"You would see yourself as I see you! You are the Righteousness of God, you are blessed with Abraham's blessings, you are free from the curse of the law, and you are delivered from the powers of darkness! You are healed by My stripes."

What a revelation began to flood my soul! The reality of God's Word in my life!

Now it may seem that all is lost! It may seem like you are going to die with this disease that is afflicting you. It may seem like you will never get out of debt. It may even seem like God does not love you anymore!

But God's Word tells you something different! God's Word tells you the truth of the situation!

What is the truth?

> *The just shall live by faith (in God's word) and not by sight!*

The truth is:

You are coming out of this situation!
(If you will believe God's Word)

Why?

Because the word of God says in *Matthew 11:28 "Come unto me all you who are heavy laden (with worries, and fears, and depression, financial trouble) and I will give you rest!* Not only will He give you rest but He watches over His Word to perform it!

He has promised to meet *all your needs according to His riches in Glory by Christ Jesus! [Phil. 4:19]*

By His stripes you are healed! [Matt. 8:17]

God so loves you that He gave His only begotten Son! [John 3:16]

Worry! What a waste of time!

What good is worry? Has it ever done you, or anyone else any good?

No! A million times No!

What is the cure for worry and fear?

Isaiah 61 says *"Put on the garment of praise for the Spirit of heaviness"* (Worry)

Begin to praise and worship God because He cannot lie!

Begin to shout the victory in the face of apparent defeat!

When you read God's eternal Word you begin to see, and know the truth.

And according to God's Word,

The truth will set you free!

Trust in the Lord with all your heart. Lean not unto your own understanding!

May I wish you all a very Happy New Year as you learn to trust God's Word!

Don't Worry! Be Happy!

Nineteen

In Jesus Name?

A decade or so ago this teaching was being taught all over the world. Since then it has almost disappeared from the pulpit! Please read this without the thought "I have heard this before!"

Read it as though it were fresh revelation! (For many it actually will be new!) Meditate on this article until the truth of it dawns on your spirit.

A number of years ago I was praying on my knees about midnight in my living room. The Lord spoke to me and said, *"Stand upright on thy feet."* I tried but could not obey. I could not stand up! (I really tried!)

Then the Lord said, *"Now stand up in Jesus Name!"* I stood up effortless, and without any exertion. The Lord then said, *"In these last days you must learn to stand in the Name of Jesus, or you will not be able to stand!"*

So I did a study on The Name of Jesus. The best book I found on the subject was (Besides the Bible!) *"The Wonderful Name of Jesus"* by E.W. Kenyon.

In this book Mr. Kenyon was giving a lecture on The Name of Jesus, when a lawyer stood up and said, "Do you mean to say that Jesus gave us the power of attorney to use His Name?"

Mr. Kenyon said, "Sir, you are a lawyer and I am just a layman, tell me, did Jesus give to the Church the Power of attorney to use His Name?

The lawyer said "If I know anything about the English language, according to the Bible, Jesus has given us this right!

Mr. Kenyon then asked, "How much power does this give to the Church?"

To which he replied, "It depends on how much power the man Himself has!"

The power of attorney simply means:
"The ability to conduct someone else's business as though He or She were here conducting the business themselves!"

Hallelujah!

To further illustrate this just suppose Bill Gates (The founder and CEO of Microsoft) were to give you his Power of attorney. All that Mr. Gates has would be at your disposal! (He is a billionaire!)

Well! ONE greater than Bill gates has come! He faced Satan and all his cohorts of hell and defeated him on his own turf! *(Colossians 2:12-15)* He actually arose from the dead! He defeated death itself and the fear of it!

In Jesus Name, we, as born again believers have the right to conduct Jesus' business on earth as if He were here conducting it Himself!

> *John 16:23*
> *Hitherto (Up 'till now) have you asked nothing in my name! Whatever you ask the Father in my name, He will give it to you!*

When we pray in Jesus Name it is as though Jesus Himself were doing the praying!

When we command a disease to leave our body, or someone else's body, in Jesus Name, it is as though Jesus Himself had given the command!

When we command satan in any shape, form or fashion, it is as though Jesus Himself were doing the commanding!

In *Matthew 28:18* we find *all power in Heaven and Earth has been given to Him!* This is the One Who has given us (you) the power of attorney to conduct His business!

> *Acts 4:12*
> *For there is none other Name under heaven given among men whereby we must be saved!*

We are saved in the Name of Jesus!

Acts 2:8 -10 We receive the Baptism in the Holy Ghost in that Name!

This is just the beginning of the use of that Glorious Name!

We can use it in our praise and worship, and in our combat with the unseen forces of satan, and in our prayer life!

Thank God for giving us the Power of attorney to use that Name!

The Wonderful Name of Jesus!

Twenty

It's February, and Almost Valentine's Day

February 14! This is a date that is set aside by the world to celebrate LOVE! Love today has many meanings! We love our cars, and chocolate ice cream! (Really.... chocolate anything!)

Lust and sex is passed off as love in many cases. Particularly in the Hollywood movies, magazines, books, etc. What a shame love has been diluted down to something dirty!

We picture little cherubim's flying around with the bows and arrows shooting young (and maybe not so young!) people as they fall in love!

This kind of love as described is unfortunately sometimes "here today and gone tomorrow!" As divorce statistics reveal to us.

But the love of God, as described in *1 Corinthians 13*, is a far more serious thing!

Even in the Christian realm Love does not carry the reality of all it suggests.

Here is a description of God's love! You will notice quite a difference between the world's love and His!

1 Corinthians 13:1-8 AMP
1 If I [can] speak in the tongues of men and [even] of an-
gels, but have not love (that reasoning, intentional, spiri-
tual devotion such [a]as is inspired by God's love for and
in us), I am only a noisy gong or a clanging cymbal.
2 And if I have prophetic powers (the gift of interpreting
the divine will and purpose), and understand all the secret
truths and mysteries and possess all knowledge, and if I have
[sufficient] faith so that I can remove mountains, but have
not love (God's love in me) I am nothing (a useless nobody).
3 Even if I dole out all that I have [to the poor in provid-
ing] food, and if I surrender my body to be burned or [c]
in order that I may glory, but have not love (God's love
in me), I gain nothing.
4 Love endures long and is patient and kind; love never
is envious nor boils over with jealousy, is not boastful or
vainglorious, does not display itself haughtily.
5 It is not conceited (arrogant and inflated with pride);
it is not rude (unmannerly) and does not act unbecom-
ingly. Love (God's love in us) does not insist on its own
rights or its own way, for it is not self-seeking; it is not
touchy or fretful or resentful; it takes no account of the
evil done to it [it pays no attention to a suffered wrong].
6 It does not rejoice at injustice and unrighteousness,
but rejoices when right and truth prevail.
7 Love bears up under anything and everything that
comes, is ever ready to believe the best of every person,
its hopes are fadeless under all circumstances, and it en-

dures everything [without weakening].
8 Love never fails [never fades out or becomes obsolete or comes to an end].

There are a lot of things mentioned in these verses of Scripture! So many in fact it would probably take a year to go through them all.

I will endeavor to go through some high lights of them, but the real meaning of them can only come to us through meditating on them, or as Jeremiah says in His book in:

Jeremiah 15:16 AMP
Your words were found, and I ate them; and Your words were to me a joy and the rejoicing of my heart, for I am called by Your name, O Lord God of hosts.

In 1 Corinthians Chapter 13 we find some of the richest, most profound teaching in the Word of God! Actually it is a measuring stick of true Christianity!

To live in this LOVE is, to me, the highest type of Christian life! God is Love! We are children of God! We are to be imitators of our Father! His love has been shed abroad in our hearts by the Holy Ghost! His love for us is unconditional!

Romans 5:5-8
5 And hope maketh not ashamed; because the love of God is shed abroad in our hearts by the Holy Ghost which is given unto us.
6 For when we were yet without strength, in due time

Christ died for the ungodly.
7 For scarcely for a righteous man will one die: yet peradventure for a good man some would even dare to die.
8 But God commendeth his love toward us, in that, while we were yet sinners Christ died for us!

Many of us think we are pretty spiritual and obedient to God's commands, until we read God's definition of LOVE!

I have seen, and known people who have "known" God for many years! They follow what they think is God's dress code, they don't do this and don't do that, but put a little pressure on them and they are just as mean, self centered, angry, greedy, foul mouthed, obnoxious, fist fighting, porno watching, backbiting, gossiping, lying, cheating, stealing (You get the picture! I am not holding back here!) as they always were! Not all of course.....but some!

I would advise new Christians (and older ones) to read and meditate on these passages in *1 Corinthians 13* at least once a day for 30 days and to begin to grasp their significance in our lives. If you will do that, you will notice a calmness, and peace begin to come over you! Your relationships will begin to take on a whole new meaning! Life will be a sweet thing instead of a continual struggle! Prayer will come easy! The atmosphere around your home will drastically change for the better! Joy will permeate the air around you!

We are admonished by God to love others.....as we love ourselves!

The trouble with many is that they have not learned to love

themselves yet!

They have not forgiven themselves for all their past sins, when God has no recollection of them!

> *Hebrews 8:12*
> *For I will be merciful to their unrighteousness, and their sins and their iniquities will I remember no more.*

The real truth is Satan flies around with his bow and arrow and uses his poison arrow (fiery darts!) of guilt to hold people down.

Basically Christians have not grasped the fact that when they were born again something happened on the inside!

> *2 Corinthians 5:17 AMP*
> *Therefore if any person is [ingrafted] in Christ (the Messiah) he is a new creation (a new creature altogether); the old [previous moral and spiritual condition] has passed away. Behold, the fresh and new has come!*

Notice the Word "NEW!" Not just forgiven, but NEW!

That person is not a forgiven sinner but a …Brand new creation….. of love!

But…in order for this love to come to the surface we must determine to give it place in our lives! Sometimes it takes a decision, and like most other change decisions it takes some work and time!

Twenty-One

My Family Tree?

John 3:1-7
1 There was a man of the Pharisees, named Nicodemus, a ruler of the Jews:
2 The same came to Jesus by night, and said unto him, Rabbi, we know that thou art a teacher come from God: for no man can do these miracles that thou doest, except God be with him.
3 Jesus answered and said unto him, Verily, verily, I say unto thee, Except a man be born again, he cannot see the kingdom of God.
4 Nicodemus saith unto him, How can a man be born when he is old? can he enter the second time into his mother's womb, and be born?
5 Jesus answered, Verily, verily, I say unto thee, Except a man be born of water and of the Spirit, he cannot enter into the kingdom of God.
6 That which is born of the flesh is flesh; and that which is born of the Spirit is spirit.
7 Marvel not that I said unto thee, Ye must be born again.

BORN AGAIN!

You were born to your natural family as someone who is

brand new! No one had seen you before! You just now came into being!

So when you heard the Gospel of Jesus Christ and you received Him as your Lord and Savior, you were Born Again! (In your spirit! The real you!)

> *2 Corinthians 5:17*
> *"Therefore if any man be in Christ, he is a new creature: old things are passed away; behold, all things are become new."*

New! Not just forgiven!

Just as you were brand new when you were born naturally, now that you have been born again, you are just as brand new in your spirit man as you were when you were born in the natural!! Praise God! Your past is gone, everything you ever did concerning sin is gone! Old things are "Passed Away!" (Dead!)

Now! When something is dead you bury it! God cast your sins as far away as "...the East is from the West!" He buried them in the "depths of the ocean"! The deepest sea!

The best thing you can do is leave them there! Do not go and dig them up!

Or as the Apostle Paul put it in :

> *Phillipians 3:13*
> *"Brethren, I count not myself to have apprehended: but this one thing I do, forgetting those things which are behind,*

and reaching forth unto those things which are before."

You must remember that Paul was responsible for the deaths of hundreds of Christians!

This new birth was so real to Paul that he declares this in:

2 Corinthians 7:2
"Receive us; we have wronged no man, we have corrupted no man, we have defrauded no man."

He could not say that about his "old man" because he did defraud them! But speaking as a new creature in Christ, as a born again man, he could make that statement of absolute truth!

So, it would do you well to do the same thing Paul did! Forget your past! It no longer exixts in God's mind!

ANOTHER TRUTH!

Now there is another truth that needs to be seen here in the new birth!

There are certain things, or traits, that occur in a family tree such as a certain illness, or fear, or anxiety, or depression, or poverty, that seem to be passed down from generation to generation! These are called "generational curses" by many. These things are reiterated, and told to you over a lifetime, by many well intentioned folks until they are believed by you and eventually brought to pass. (Unless you put a stop to them)

Let me give you an example!

Let's say a certain family is plagued with heart trouble, and grandfather, and dad died early in life because of this. You have been told all your life by relatives that you must take it easy because your grandfather died at 48, and your dad died at 43, so you must be on the look out for high blood pressure, and heart trouble!

So how do most people respond? The first think is fear, or anxiety, that you will probably have this also! Satan backs up those fears with small symptoms from time to time, and the fear increases. Jesus said that in the last days men's hearts will fail them "because of fear"! So one of the very things that causes heart trouble is set into motion! And if paid heed to, and feared, and believed long enough it can cause to come to pass what never would have occurred if you knew the truth!

WHAT IS THE TRUTH?

> *John 8:31-32*
> *30 As he spake these words, many believed on him.*
> *31 Then said Jesus to those Jews which believed on him, If ye continue in my word, then are ye my disciples indeed;* (Make His Word your final authority!)
> *32 And ye shall know the truth, and the truth shall make you free.*

So! What is the truth about your family tree, according to God's Word?

You are a "Born again" person, and so you have a new family tree!

God is now your Father, Jesus is now your brother, and neither one of them has heart trouble, or cancer, or anxiety, or depression, and they are not broke, so YOU DON'T HAVE TO RECEIVE THESE THINGS EITHER!

You have a new "birth right" to be healthy, at peace, and blessed financially!

Stand up for your rights and shout at the devil "I am not having this devil!" It is all under the curse according to *Deuteronomy 28!*

> *Galatians 3:13*
> *"Christ has redeemed me from the curse of the law."*

Now! You have found out the truth!

Now! What will you do with it? ...Hint!

> *James 4: 7*
> *Submit yourselves therefore to God. (Believe His Word and it will set you free!) (then) Resist the devil, and he will flee from you.*

RISE UP! DO IT!

Twenty-Two

Our Compassionate Father

Jeremiah 9:23-24
23 Thus saith the Lord, Let not the wise man glory in his wisdom, neither let the mighty man glory in his might, let not the rich man glory in his riches.
24 But let him that glorieth, glory in this, that he understandeth and knoweth Me, that I Am the Lord which exercise loving-kindness, judgment, and righteousness in the Earth: for in these things I delight saith the Lord.

In these verses God is inviting us to get to know Him!! What an invitation!! What a real blessing, knowing God! Our number One priority should be to know our heavenly Father! Time spent getting to know Him is time well spent! Not just knowing about Him, but REALLY know Him!

There are many misconceptions about God out there, not only in the world, but in the church world as well. Let me say something I heard the Spirit of the Lord say one day! He said "Your future is as bright as your conception of God!"

Many people have the idea that God is sitting on His throne looking down on Earth thinking of ways to keep people out of Heaven, and how to make and keep them sick, and causing them to lie down so they will look up. How to keep them from having anything but the bare minimum! But nothing could be farther from the truth!

Jesus said in *John 8:31-32*

> *31 If you continue in My Word, then are you my disciples indeed;*
> *32 and you shall know the Truth, and the truth shall make you free!!*

So if we want to know the truth about God we will find it in the Word! (Desciple means a disciplined one)

First of all let's look at *Psalms 145:8-9* and get a true picture of God.

The Lord is gracious (disposed to show favors) full of compassion (to love tenderly, to pity, to show mercy, to be full of eager yearning) slow to anger, and of great mercy. The Lord is good to all, and His tender mercies are over all His works! This is a word picture of our heavenly Father!

> *John 1:1*
> *In the beginning was the Word, and the Word was with God and the Word was God!*

Hallelujah!

I would like to look at one aspect of the Word Compassion. It means to be full of eager yearning. You may ask, "What does that have to do with compassion?" It simply means that He is full of eager yearning to fulfill all of His Great and Precious promises to His faithful children, and to this lost and dying world!

For instance when you buy your child a Christmas gift in October and you have to wait for Christmas to give it to him! Full of eager yearning is the way you feel between October and December 25!! His benevolent heart is looking for ways to get His provided blessings to His children!

If you really want to get an accurate picture of God, all you have to do is take the hand of Jesus and walk with Him through Matthew, Mark, Luke, and John!

Jesus said in John 14:7 If you had known me you would have known my Father also. In John 10:30 He said "my father and I are ONE !" So let's have a look at Jesus in a few Scriptures and learn of our Father!

> *Mark 1:40-42*
> *40 There came a leper to Him (Jesus), beseeching Him and kneeling down to Him, and saying to Him, if thou wilt, thou canst make me clean.*
> *41 And Jesus moved with compassion, put forth His hand, and touched Him, and saith unto him "I will be thou clean."*
> *42 And as soon as He had spoken, immediately the Leprosy departed from him, and he was cleansed!*

Praise the Lord, for He is Good! God is not anything so much as He is Love! In fact the Word says in *1 John 4:8* ***GOD IS***

LOVE !!! In the case of this leper, and every other case in the Bible God's Love was **UNCONDITIONAL!** It did not matter if this was an outcast of society, or had no money, or did not dress in fine clothes, or what color or gender he was!! God just loved Him and was full of eager yearning to bless him!

In *Matthew 14:14* we find another instance of the Lords compassion!

> *And Jesus went forth and saw a great multitude, and was Moved with compassion toward them, and healed there sick!!*

Glory to God!

Again I would like to emphasize that God's Love was **UNCONDITIONAL!** If you think about it you know that there was some people in that crowd who had done wrong, sinful things that day! But He loved them just the same! At the same time you must remember that none of them were born again, because the new birth was not available at that time! Jesus had not gone to the cross yet!

Sometimes I think that the reason that this kind of love is so hard to grasp is that we have nothing to compare it to! In the English language we have a limited vocabulary when it comes to Love! We say we love our dog, and that we love ice cream, then we turn around and say we love our wives or husbands! In the Greek language there were several words used for Love and they are very helpful in the use of the word. One of the words is *Phileo*, which is the highest kind of love that man can produce in his own efforts. This word is the reason divorce lawyers are rich! It is based almost entirely on the performance of your mate! As long as dinner is on the table, on time and my shirts are ironed, and the house is cleaned I will love you! But cross me and you will see what happens! At the altar phileo says "I'll love you to the end!" Six months later it says, "This is the end!"

The Greek word for God's Love is '*Agape.*' It is absolutely unconditional! It is not in any way based on your performance, but on the goodness of God! Nothing, not even hell can separate you from the love of God, which is in Christ Jesus!

This brings us to the greatest act of Love ever known to mankind! It is found in *John 3:16* where *God so loved the world that He gave His only begotten Son, that whosoever believeth in Him shall not perish, but have everlasting life!*

Praise God! In this Scripture God does the unthinkable! He sacrifices His own beloved Son for you and I! I wonder if any of us has plumbed the depths of this Greatest of all Love?

Now why did God do this? To see His Son beaten beyond recognition? To see Him spat upon, and humiliated, and crowned with thorns? Nailed to an old rugged cross?

> *Romans 5:8*
> *God commended (proved) His love toward us in that while we were yet sinners Christ died for us!!!*

Now you know a little more about our wonderful Heavenly

Father! When you truly know Him, the struggle for faith is over! The Apostle Paul said *"I know whom I have believed, and am persuaded that He is able to keep what I have committed to Him against that day!"*

To know Him is to love Him!! God loves you with an everlasting, unconditional love! The Lord said to me one day that "as I prayed for the sick I was to tell them He loved to heal them!" Many people have the mistaken idea that we have to Talk Him into the notion of healing them! But you see the truth is that He took those stripes so you could be healed!

Healing as well as forgiveness and prosperity have already been provided through Jesus' death burial and resurrection! All that God requires of you is to believe, and receive His provisions! Everything that God does for humanity stems from the fact that He *so loved the world that He gave His only begotten Son.*

Praise His Name forever!

Twenty-Three

Overcoming Discouragement

Discouragement - (To terrorize, to take away courage, to paralyze partially or wholly, to deactivate from action); -- other words for discouraged. Hopeless, depressed, despondent, joyless.

Encouragement - (To impart courage, to strengthen, to lift up, to cause joy)

Discouragement is one of satan's main weapons against the born again child of God! It is a hideous thing sent from hell to bring the Christian to his emotional knees! This demonic influence when in it's most severe stages may cause suicidal thoughts to come to overwhelm even Spirit-filled Christians.

Many Reasons, Or For No Known Reason

Indeed there are thousands of scenarios that open the door to discouragement. The loss of employment, divorce, unpaid bills, friends turning their back on you, the way your body looks (ie. to skinny, too fat, etc. etc), sickness, fear. Why aren't my kids serving God? I must be a failure as a parent.

We could go on and on, but I think you get the idea!

Satan will try to get you to think you are the only one going through this! If you had any faith this would not be happening to you. Remember he is a liar, a deceiver, and the Accuser of the brethren.

No matter who you are there are times when everyone is tempted with discouragement. Sometimes for days, or weeks, the battle goes on. Life does not seem to have any joy, it is a constant battle! Sometimes the person being attacked does not even know why they are discouraged! And sometimes there is no earthly reason for these dark feelings. They are just being attacked by satan.

The believer is attacked with a sense of purposelessness. Hopelessness. Fear. Depression. Doubt. A feeling as though God has turned His back on you.

Remember

It is in times like these we need to remember God's Word. We need to ask ourselves "What does God say about what's going on?" We need to remember the faithfulness of God in our past experience. Remember what God has brought you through in days gone by! Rehearse them over and over again in your mind! Make a list of these things, and read them out loud to yourself, to God, and to the devil! Count your blessings! Always remember that God is with you and on your side, and that He loves you with an unfailing, unconditional love!

Many of the heroes of faith in the Bible were tempted to be discouraged!

Even King David as you read the Psalms you see his battles with discouragement!

We find him speaking to his own soul (mind) in...

> *Psalms 42:5*
> *"Why art thou cast down O my soul, and why art thou disquieted (discouraged) in me? Hope thou in God: for I shall yet praise Him for the help of His countenance!*

This is King David in an obvious time of discouragement! But see how He handles it! He speaks to his own mind and tells it to take courage! And he speaks his faith saying the end result of this dark time will be his praising God for His help! Kathryn Kuhlman said these words, "In the light of all Jesus has accomplished, what's left but praise?"

Notice David's cure for the downcast soul "I will yet praise Him in advance of the manifested victory because I know God is for me and I can not lose!"

Sometimes when there is no one else around to encourage you, you must learn to encourage yourself! Rise up and begin to speak God's Word! Begin to shout unto God with the voice of triumph! If God be for you, who can stand against you! Begin to praise God with your whole being! Not for the problem, but in spite of it! And watch discouragement, and the devil behind it, flee!

James 4:7
Submit yourself to God! Resist the devil, and he will flee (run in terror) from you!

As the song says,

"It Is No Secret what God can do,
what He's done for others He'll do for you.

With arms wide open, He'll pardon you,
It is no secret what God can do!

Twenty-Four

Praise! The Language of Faith!

Hebrews 11:6
But without faith it is impossible to please him: for he that cometh to God must believe that he is, and that he is a rewarder of them that diligently seek him.

Hebrews 11:6 The Message
It's impossible to please God apart from faith. And why? Because anyone who wants to approach God must believe both that he exists and that he cares enough to respond to those who seek him.

Note! It is impossible to PLEASE Him without faith! Remember that phrase as we go along in this study!

I am going to share with you one of the greatest things I have discovered about living by faith, and releasing your faith.

Psalms 69:30-31
30 I will praise the name of God with a song, and will magnify him with thanksgiving.
31 This also shall PLEASE the LORD better than an ox or bullock that hath horns and hoofs.

Now consider this:

Matthew 4:4
But he answered and said, It is written, Man shall not live by bread alone, but by every word that proceedeth out of the mouth of God.

"To live" by the Word means to act upon the Word!

Or as James puts it in his book...

Janes 1:22
But be ye doers of the word, and not hearers only, deceiving your own selves.

James 2:17
Even so faith, if it hath not works, is dead, being alone.

James 2:17 AMP
So also faith, if it does not have works (deeds and actions of obedience to back it up), by itself is destitute of power (inoperative, dead).

Or as someone said **"Faith without corresponding actions is dead!"**

So if the Psalmist who wrote this is right (and he was because every Scripture is inspired by the Holy Ghost!) then Praise has got something to do with faith!

Praise is one way of having corresponding actions with the Word! It is acting as though God's Word were true!

There is only one excuse in the Bible for not praising the Lord! It is found in:

> *Psalms 115:17*
> *The dead praise not the Lord, neither any who go down into silence.*

Now I don't know about you but I do not qualify for that group!

The Lord gave me several reasons for praise, and the results of praise!

1. Praise releases faith!
2. Praise is the atmosphere God lives in! *[Ps 22:3]*
3. Praise is a type of meditation in the Word! *[Jos 1:8]*
4. Praise will renew your mind, will and emotions! *[Ro 12:2]*
5. Praise will renew your strength! *[Is 40:29-31]*
6. Praise closes Satan's mouth! *[Ps 8:2]*
7. Praise will increase the anointing!
8. Praise will bring miracles and deliverance! *[2 Chr 20]*
9. Praise takes your mind off the problem and fixes it on God!

These are some of the benefits of praising the Lord! (Even before an answer to prayer is manifest!)

Praise is the language of faith! If you must learn a new language try the language of faith!

Twenty-Five

Praise, Worship, and Thanksgiving!

These words have been coming up in my spirit for many days now. In fact I started teaching a series on this subject at our church on Wednesday nights for the past 4 weeks, and will continue for a few more weeks at the Lord's direction.

I was in a Sunday through Sunday meeting in Ohio years ago. (Remember those?) The meeting gained in attendance every night until there were those sitting in the foyer!

When I asked the Lord what I was supposed to teach on the first Sunday morning the answer came immediately "I want you to teach on praise and worship all week."

Well that startled me because as I carefully explained to the Lord "I don't know that much about that subject to speak for a whole week on it!"

He answered ***"I know it! And neither do they!"*** (The Congregation)

He went on to say ***"I will teach you in the daytime, so you can teach them what I teach you at night time!"***

Well the first Sunday morning I launched out into the "unknown"!

I announced the subject for the week and thought I heard a few moans from the people.

One couple told me and the pastor after the first service that they did not like all this singing of Biblical choruses,.... they wanted to go back to the old hymn books. (This took place back when the Church first began singing choruses.) And they did not like all the teaching on praise.

Well, just to show you the effect of a weeks teaching on the subject, these same people were dancing in the aisles at the last few services! (True!)

The Lord has been reminding me of these services and said it was time to teach it again.

So in obedience to Him here we go!

John 19:1
"Then Pilate therefore took Jesus, and scourged him."

We have failed to understand the full extent of this verse.

Let's look at what the Bible says about this event hundreds of years before it took place.

Isaiah 52:14 AMP
[For many the Servant of God became an object of hor-

ror; many were astonished at Him.] His face and His whole appearance were marred more than any man's, and His form beyond that of the sons of men--but just as many were astonished at Him....

The soldiers literally beat Him beyond recognition. Mel Gibson did a marvelous job of depicting this scene in his movie "The Passion."

They made Jesus carry the cross to Golgotha Hill. (Actually He fell under the weight of it because of His weakened condition from blood loss, and the soldiers told a stranger to help Him)

When they reached the hill itself they disrobed Him and laid Him naked on a cross. They proceeded to drive spikes through His hands and feet. Then the raised His naked body on the cross for all to see and dropped it into a hole in the ground.

Psalms 22:1
My God, my God, why hast thou forsaken me? Why art thou so far from helping me, and from the words of my roaring?

These are the Words of Jesus as He hung there a bleeding mass of flesh.

Here we see a picture of this as prophesied by David many years before it happened.

Now look in the 14th and 15th and 17th verse.

14 I am poured out like water, and all my bones are out of joint: my heart is like wax; it is melted in the midst of my bowels.
15 My strength is dried up like a potsherd; and my tongue cleaveth to my jaws; and thou hast brought me into the dust of death.
17 I may tell all my bones: they look and stare upon me.

He could actually see His bones protruding through the beaten flesh. Just before He died He said...

"IT IS FINISHED!"

In John the 17th chapter He had said, *"I have finished the work you gave me to do!"*..... (Destroying the works of the devil, and substituting for the sin and sickness, and poverty of mankind in His death.)

When He spoke those Words it meant, ***"All the work I came to do while on earth is finished!"***

Isaiah 53:4-6 AMP
4 Surely He has borne our griefs (sicknesses, weaknesses, and distresses) and carried our sorrows and pains [of punishment], yet we [ignorantly] considered Him stricken, smitten, and afflicted by God [as if with leprosy].
5 But He was wounded for our transgressions, He was bruised for our guilt and iniquities; the chastisement [needful to obtain] peace and well-being for us was upon Him, and with the stripes [that wounded] Him we are healed and made whole.

6 All we like sheep have gone astray, we have turned every one to his own way; and the Lord has made to light upon Him the guilt and iniquity of us all

Hallelujah!

He did all that was necessary for our cleansing from sin, and gave us His peace (mental and spiritual stability), and physical healing!

Since He did it all, what kind of praise, worship and thanksgiving, should we be giving God the Father for His great plan of salvation?!!

Katherine Kuhlman once said, "In the light of what Jesus has already accomplished.....what's left but praise?" Glory to God!

The Lord spoke to me recently and said, ***"Enter into praise, worship and thanksgiving and I will take care of the rest!"***

Glory to God!!

Twenty-Six

Reasons to Praise Him!

Psalms 34:1-4
1 I will bless the LORD at all times: his praise shall continually be in my mouth.
2 My soul shall make her boast in the LORD: the humble shall hear thereof, and be glad.
3 O magnify the LORD with me, and let us exalt his name together.
4 I sought the LORD, and he heard me, and delivered me from all my fears.

Well! I don't know what everyone is getting so excited about!

Psalms 150:1-6
1 Praise ye the LORD. Praise God in his sanctuary: praise him in the firmament of his power.
2 Praise him for his mighty acts: praise him according to his excellent greatness.
3 Praise him with the sound of the trumpet: praise him with the psaltery and harp.
4 Praise him with the timbrel and dance: praise him with stringed instruments and organs.
5 Praise him upon the loud cymbals: praise him upon

the high sounding cymbals.
6 Let everything that hath breath praise the LORD. Praise ye the LORD.

Many say "Well! I can't think of any reasons to praise Him?" "Peace in the Valley is their favorite song! It starts out "Well I'm so tired and so weary….."

Poor old me! Nobody knows the trouble I've seen!

How about this for a reason?

Because we are commanded to!!

Not only that, but here are some reasons to praise Him if you are running out!

He created the heavens and the earth, and galaxies.
But what has He done for me personally?

Praise Him for:
The air you breathe!
The clothes you wear.
The food you eat!
The car you drive.
The house you live in!
The liquid you drink!
The new birth.
For making heaven your home not hell!
The baptism in the Holy Spirit.
For your family!

Your pets!
Your Health!
Your ability to walk, talk, see, hear, smell, taste, and feel!
The strength to work and bless your family!
Beautiful days, the sunshine and the rain!
Because You live in a free country!
The flowers, trees, grass, ….etc etc etc
Then when your finished doing that!

Praise Him for Who He is!

He is the Elohim of Genesis! The protector of Shadrach, Meshach, and Abednego, He is the One Who guided the stone from David's sling shot into Goliath's forehead.

He is the I am of Moses, the El Shaddai of Abraham!

He is the Alpha and Omega, The Lamb of God, The Son of God, the Rose of Sharon, The Lily of the valley, The Living Word of God, The Prince of Peace, the Wonderful Counselor, the Everlasting Father, Our Savior, Healer, Righteousness, Provider, our Victor, and victory, God Almighty!

He walked on the water, fed 5000 with 2 fish and 5 loaves, He healed the sick, raised the dead, cast out devils, He is the Bread of Life, the Father of Mercies, He is Unconditional Love incarnate!

He was beaten to a pulp, was crucified, He died on a cross, was pierced by a Roman spear, went to hell, suffered all hell had to offer, but on the third day He arose from the dead, victorious over death hell and the grave. He has the keys of death and hell, He was alive, then was dead, then alive forevermore!

He is seated at the Father's right hand making intercession for you right now!

He is our advocate, the Door to Heaven,
The Way the Truth and the Life!
The Lion of the tribe of Judah.

Revelations 5:1-14
1 And I saw in the right hand of him that sat on the
throne a book written within and on the backside,
sealed with seven seals.
2 And I saw a strong angel proclaiming with a loud
voice, Who is worthy to open the book, and to loose the
seals thereof?
3 And no man in heaven, nor in earth, neither under the
earth, was able to open the book, neither to look thereon.
4 And I wept much, because no man was found worthy
to open and to read the book, neither to look thereon.
5 And one of the elders saith unto me, Weep not: behold,
the Lion of the tribe of Judah, the Root of David, hath pre-
vailed to open the book, and to loose the seven seals thereof.
6 And I beheld, and, lo, in the midst of the throne and of the
four beasts, and in the midst of the elders, stood a Lamb as
it had been slain, having seven horns and seven eyes, which
are the seven Spirits of God sent forth into all the earth.
7 And he came and took the book out of the right hand
of him that sat upon the throne.
8 And when he had taken the book, the four beasts and

four and twenty elders fell down before the Lamb, having every one of them harps, and golden vials full of odours, which are the prayers of saints.
9 And they sung a new song, saying, Thou art worthy to take the book, and to open the seals thereof: for thou wast slain, and hast redeemed us to God by thy blood out of every kindred, and tongue, and people, and nation;
10 And hast made us unto our God kings and priests: and we shall reign on the earth.
11 And I beheld, and I heard the voice of many angels round about the throne and the beasts and the elders: and the number of them was ten thousand times ten thousand, and thousands of thousands;
12 Saying with a loud voice, Worthy is the Lamb that was slain to receive power, and riches, and wisdom, and strength, and honour, and glory, and blessing.
13 And every creature which is in heaven, and on the earth, and under the earth, and such as are in the sea, and all that are in them, heard I saying, Blessing, and honour, and glory, and power, be unto him that sitteth upon the throne, and unto the Lamb for ever and ever.
14 And the four beasts said, Amen. And the four and twenty elders fell down and worshipped him that liveth for ever and ever.

Well I wonder if He is worthy of our Praise worship and Thanksgiving! Reason Enough?

Shout Hallelujah Somebody!!!!!

Twenty-Seven

Rejoice and Count It Done (Part 1)

While attending 'Prayer & Healing School' at RHEMA Bible Training Center, Brother Kenneth Hagin brought forth a Word from the Lord to the whole congregation.

This was the Word:

> *"The winds of good shall begin to blow upon the sails of the ship of your life, and they shall carry you into the harbor of tranquility, and serenity, and no longer shall there be agitation in your emotional realm. But the peace of God shall surmount your entire being! And you will say This is it! This is the Way!"*

At the end of that Word from the Lord The Holy Spirit said through him, ***"I want you to Rejoice and Count It Done! Hallelujah!"***

This is a great way to exercise your faith! Whatever it is you are believing God for, if you can find a promise for it in the Scriptures, you can just give your petition to God in prayer, then after prayer from that time on, just rejoice and count it done!

FINAL AUTHORITY!

To do this successfully you must make God's Word your final authority!

Remember that:

Numbers 23:19
God is not a man that He should lie, neither the son of man that He should repent. Has He said and will He not do it? Has He spoken and shall it not come to pass?

John 1:1
"In the beginning was the Word, and the Word was with God and the Word was God."

We must learn to give the Word of God the same place we would give Jesus if He was here in the flesh speaking directly to us!!

Mark 11:24
"What things soever you desire, when you pray, believe that you receive them, and you shall have them."

If you have been a Christian very long you know that there is usually a time period between the time that you believe that you receive them.........and you shall have them!

Got Confidence?

It's during that time when you must decide if you have any confidence in God or not!

It is during that time that the devil will try his best to talk you out of what you are believing God for!

The way you think, talk, and act during that period, will determine whether you receive it (the answer to your prayer) or not! <u>This is where we must show God we have faith!</u>

How do we show God our faith?

The Bible says in *Matthew 9* referring to the four men who let their paralyzed friend down through the roof *"When He saw their faith!"* Thank God faith can be seen! It's not enough to say you have faith, you must let your faith be seen! We know that God has said that He would never leave us nor forsake us, so we know His eye is always on us, watching us! Now I would like to ask you a question!

What is He seeing in you?

Is He seeing your faith, or are you projecting doubt and unbelief in the way you think talk and act?

How do we Act?

How are we to act between the time that you believe that you receive them,...and you shall have them? Well my best answer to that was what the Holy Spirit said through Brother Hagin, ***"I want you to rejoice and count it done!"*** Just rejoice and count it done!!

Is this principle used in the Bible?

Oh Yes! Check out this Scripture!

Habakkuk 3:17-18
17 Although the fig tree shall not blossom, neither shall fruit be in the vines; the labor of the olive shall fail, and the fields shall yield no meat; the flock shall be cut off from the fold, and there shall be no herd in the stalls;
18 Yet I will rejoice in the Lord; I will joy in the God of my salvation!!

Here we have a man that has almost nothing in this material world, no food, and nothing in sight to give him hope, but he says, "Yet I will rejoice in the Lord!"

Now why, and how can this man rejoice?

Because he has God's Word that He will be his Provider! His strength and His song! He knows that these dire circumstances are subject to change! So he rejoices and counts it done! God will lift him above this temporary set back!

We have another example of this in:

2 Chronicles 20:1-22
1 It came to pass after this also, that the children of Moab, and the children of Ammon, and with them other beside the Ammonites, came against Jehoshaphat to battle.
2 Then there came some that told Jehoshaphat, saying, There cometh a great multitude against thee from beyond the sea on this side Syria; and, behold, they be in

Hazazontamar, which is Engedi.
3 And Jehoshaphat feared, and set himself to seek the
LORD, and proclaimed a fast throughout all Judah.
4 And Judah gathered themselves together, to ask help of
the LORD: even out of all the cities of Judah they came
to seek the LORD.
5 And Jehoshaphat stood in the congregation of Judah
and Jerusalem, in the house of the LORD, before the
new court,
6 And said, O LORD God of our fathers, art not thou
God in heaven? and rulest not thou over all the kingdoms of the heathen? and in thine hand is there not
power and might, so that none is able to withstand thee?
7 Art not thou our God, who didst drive out the inhabitants of this land before thy people Israel, and gavest it to
the seed of Abraham thy friend for ever?
8 And they dwelt therein, and have built thee a sanctuary therein for thy name, saying,
9 If, when evil cometh upon us, as the sword, judgment,
or pestilence, or famine, we stand before this house, and
in thy presence, (for thy name is in this house,) and cry
unto thee in our affliction, then thou wilt hear and help.
10 And now, behold, the children of Ammon and Moab
and mount Seir, whom thou wouldest not let Israel in-
vade, when they came out of the land of Egypt, but they
turned from them, and destroyed them not;
11 Behold, I say, how they reward us, to come to cast
us out of thy possession, which thou hast given us to in-
herit.
12 O our God, wilt thou not judge them? for we have no
might against this great company that cometh against us;

neither know we what to do: but our eyes are upon thee.
13 And all Judah stood before the LORD, with their little ones, their wives, and their children.
14 Then upon Jahaziel the son of Zechariah, the son of Benaiah, the son of Jeiel, the son of Mattaniah, a Levite of the sons of Asaph, came the Spirit of the LORD in the midst of the congregation;
15 And he said, Hearken ye, all Judah, and ye inhabitants of Jerusalem, and thou king Jehoshaphat, Thus saith the LORD unto you, Be not afraid nor dismayed by reason of this great multitude; for the battle is not yours, but God's.
16 To morrow go ye down against them: behold, they come up by the cliff of Ziz; and ye shall find them at the end of the brook, before the wilderness of Jeruel.
17 Ye shall not need to fight in this battle: set yourselves, stand ye still, and see the salvation of the LORD with you, O Judah and Jerusalem: fear not, nor be dismayed; to morrow go out against them: for the LORD will be with you.
18 And Jehoshaphat bowed his head with his face to the ground: and all Judah and the inhabitants of Jerusalem fell before the LORD, worshipping the LORD.
19 And the Levites, of the children of the Kohathites, and of the children of the Korhites, stood up to praise the LORD God of Israel with a loud voice on high.
20 And they rose early in the morning, and went forth into the wilderness of Tekoa: and as they went forth, Jehoshaphat stood and said, Hear me, O Judah, and ye inhabitants of Jerusalem; Believe in the LORD your God, so shall ye be established; believe his prophets, so

shall ye prosper.
21 And when he had consulted with the people, he appointed singers unto the LORD, and that should praise the beauty of holiness, as they went out before the army, and to say, Praise the LORD; for his mercy endureth for ever.
22 And when they began to sing and to praise, the LORD set ambushments against the children of Ammon, Moab, and mount Seir, which were come against Judah; and they were smitten.

Notice that it was when they began to sing and praise that the Lord intervened! By singing and praise they were rejoicing and counting what the Lord said through the prophet, DONE!

So if Satan has come against you with sickness, poverty, depression, failure, or whatever:

Find yourself a Scripture that promises you deliverance, speak it out to God, then Rejoice and count it done!!

Remember! God Cannot Lie!

Twenty-Eight

Rejoice! You Are a Child of The King!

Philippians 4:4
Rejoice in the Lord always: and again I say, Rejoice.

What a Word the apostle Paul gives us in this verse! Especially when you consider all the things Satan was bringing his way at the time!

2 Corinthians 11:25-27
25 Thrice was I beaten with rods, once was I stoned, thrice I suffered shipwreck, a night and a day I have been in the deep;
26 In journeyings often, in perils of waters, in perils of robbers, in perils by mine own countrymen, in perils by the heathen, in perils in the city, in perils in the wilderness, in perils in the sea, in perils among false brethren;
27 In weariness and painfulness, in watchings often, in hunger and thirst, in fastings often, in cold and nakedness.

Let's look at some of the reasons Paul could write in such an optimistic manner after all this in *Philippians 4:4!*

John 3:1-3
1 There was a man of the Pharisees, named Nicodemus, a ruler of the Jews:
2 The same came to Jesus by night, and said unto him, Rabbi, we know that thou art a teacher come from God: for no man can do these miracles that thou doest, except God be with him.
3 Jesus answered and said unto him, Verily, verily, I say unto thee, Except a man be born again, he cannot see the kingdom of God.

What happens when a person gets Born Again?

2 Corinthians 5:17 AMP
Therefore if any man (Person) be in Christ, (Born Again) he is a new creature: old things are passed away; behold, all things are become new. (Including the kingdom he belongs to!)

When a person is born again they come into God's family!

Colossians 1:12-13
12 Giving thanks unto the Father, which hath made us meet (able) to be partakers of the inheritance of the saints in light:
13 Who hath delivered us from the power of darkness, and hath translated us into the kingdom of his dear Son:

That person is now a child of the King! Bone of His bone and flesh of His flesh!

1 Corinthians 6:17
But he that is joined unto the Lord is one spirit.

That person is also an heir of God, and a joint-heir with Christ.

Romans 8:16-17
16 The Spirit itself beareth witness with our spirit, that we are the children of God:
17 And if children, then heirs; heirs of God, and joint-heirs with Christ;

Hallelujah! What an inheritance we have come into as actual children of God Almighty!

All that He has is now ours!

Ephesians 1:3
Blessed be the God and Father of our Lord Jesus Christ, who hath blessed us with allspiritual blessings in heavenly places in Christ:

Ephesians 1:11a
In whom also we have obtained an inheritance...

It reminds me of the Elder Brother in the story of 'the prodigal son!'

Luke 15:11-32
11 And he said, A certain man had two sons:
12 And the younger of them said to his father, Father,

give me the portion of goods that falleth to me. And he
divided unto them his living.
13 And not many days after the younger son gathered
all together, and took his journey into a far country, and
there wasted his substance with riotous living.
14 And when he had spent all, there arose a mighty fam-
ine in that land; and he began to be in want.
15 And he went and joined himself to a citizen of that
country; and he sent him into his fields to feed swine.
16 And he would fain have filled his belly with the husks
that the swine did eat: and no man gave unto him.
17 And when he came to himself, he said, How many
hired servants of my father's have bread enough and to
spare, and I perish with hunger!
18 I will arise and go to my father, and will say unto him,
Father, I have sinned against heaven, and before thee,
19 And am no more worthy to be called thy son: make
me as one of thy hired servants.
20 And he arose, and came to his father. But when he was
yet a great way off, his father saw him, and had compas-
sion, and ran, and fell on his neck, and kissed him.
21 And the son said unto him, Father, I have sinned
against heaven, and in thy sight, and am no more wor-
thy to be called thy son.
22 But the father said to his servants, Bring forth the
best robe, and put it on him; and put a ring on his hand,
and shoes on his feet:
23 And bring hither the fatted calf, and kill it; and let us
eat, and be merry:
24 For this my son was dead, and is alive again; he was
lost, and is found. And they began to be merry.

25 Now his elder son was in the field: and as he came and drew nigh to the house, he heard musick and dancing.
26 And he called one of the servants, and asked what these things meant.
27 And he said unto him, Thy brother is come; and thy father hath killed the fatted calf, because he hath received him safe and sound.
28 And he was angry, and would not go in: therefore came his father out, and intreated him.
29 And he answering said to his father, Lo, these many years do I serve thee, neither transgressed I at any time thy commandment: and yet thou never gavest me a kid, that I might make merry with my friends: (Can you hear the whine in his voice?)
30 But as soon as this thy son was come, which hath devoured thy living with harlots, thou hast killed for him the fatted calf. (Can you hear the whine in his voice?)
31 And he said unto him, Son, thou art ever with me, and all that I have is thine.

This elder brother was so busy with his duties he forgot the whole farm and everything on it was already his!

Don't get so busy about your God given "Farm" (religion) that you forget all the inherited benefits!

Thank God! We are not just going to get our inheritance when we "All get to heaven"! It's ours now!!

Healing, Peace, Deliverance, Prosperity, Joy, Strength, Wisdom, Houses, Lands, etc...

Come and get it by faith! It's Yours!!

So Rejoice! Rejoice! Rejoice!You are a child of the King!!

All that He has is Yours!

Twenty-Nine

Religion vs. Tradition

This month I would like to speak to you about a real threat to Bible-believing churches. It is called religious tradition, we will look at how it stacks up against the Word of God.

> *Mark 7:1-8 The Message*
> *1-4 The Pharisees, along with some religious scholars who had come from Jerusalem, gathered around him. They noticed that some of his disciples weren't being careful with ritual washings before meals. The Pharisees—Jews in general, in fact—would never eat a meal without going through the motions of a ritual hand-washing, with an especially vigorous scrubbing if they had just come from the market (to say nothing of the scourings they'd give jugs and pots and pans).*
> *5 The Pharisees and religious scholars asked, "Why do your disciples flout the rules, showing up at meals without washing their hands?"*
> *6-8 Jesus answered, "Isaiah was right about frauds like you, hit the bull's-eye in fact: These people make a big show of saying the right thing, but their heart isn't in it. They act like they are worshiping me, but they don't mean it.*
> *They just use me as a cover for teaching whatever suits*

their fancy, Ditching God's command and taking up the latest fads."

9 -13 He went on, "Well, good for you. You get rid of God's command so you won't be inconvenienced in following the religious fashions!.... You do a lot of things like this."

You can see Jesus was not too fond of dead religion, especially when it tries to take the place of the Living Word!

I am going to make this just as simple as I can. And hopefully set some precious people of God Free!

John 8:31-32 KJV
31 So Jesus said to those Jews who had believed in Him, If you abide in My word [hold fast to My teachings and live in accordance with them], you are truly My disciples.
32 And you will know the Truth, and the Truth will set you free.

The Truth (God's Word) will make you free from all the lies and distortions of religious tradition. Jesus came to "set the captives free!" If the Truth will make you free, that suggests you are being held captive by a lie!

Q. What does religious tradition say about sickness, disease and poor health in general?

A. Sickness is for God's glory!

O.K.! Let's analyze that for a moment. If sickness is for God's glory, then Jesus did not hesitate to rob God of all the Glory He could…He healed the sick.

Jesus said in *John 10:30 "The Father and I are One!"*

In *John 14:7-11*

> *7 "If ye had known me, ye should have known my Father also: and from henceforth ye know him, and have seen him.*
> *8 Philip saith unto him, Lord, show us the Father, and it sufficeth us.*
> *9 Jesus saith unto him, Have I been so long time with you, and yet hast thou not known me, Philip? he that hath seen me hath seen the Father; and how sayest thou then, Show us the Father?*
> *10 Believest thou not that I am in the Father, and the Father in me? the words that I speak unto you I speak not of myself: but the Father that dwelleth in me, he doeth the works.*
> *11 Believe me that I am in the Father, and the Father in me: or else believe me for the very works' sake.*

So we see in healing the sick that Jesus was acting in concert with His Father God! Doing His will! So we can deduct from this that healing must be, and is, God's will for all!

That means you dear Christian! Sickness is trying to steal from you, kill you and destroy you!

> *John 10:10*
> *"The thief (Satan) cometh not, but for to steal, and to*

kill, and to destroy: I am come that they might have life, and that they might have it more abundantly."

Sickness will steal your joy, money, faith, and anything else you can think of as far as health.

What are we to do?

REBEL against all sickness, as it comes from Satan, not God! So many folks are being destroyed from a lack of knowledge! *(Hoses 4:6)*

> *James 4:7*
> *Submit your selves therefore to God. Resist (fight, combat, rise up against)........ the devil, and he will flee from you.!*

God said he would!

How do you "resist the devil" Do it just like Jesus did! Say "It is written" then quote a Scripture that promises you deliverance, and healing from your situation!

Read *Psalms 103:1-5*

> *1 Bless the Lord, O my soul: and all that is within me, bless his holy name.*
> *2 Bless the Lord, O my soul, and forget not all his benefits:*
> *3 Who forgiveth all thine iniquities; who healeth all thy diseases;*
> *4 Who redeemeth thy life from destruction; who*

crowneth thee with lovingkindness and tender mercies;
5 Who satisfieth thy mouth with good things; so that thy youth is renewed like the eagle's.

Do it! Take the time to look these Scriptures up! How bad do you want to be made well? Then Do it!

James 1:21-22
21 Wherefore lay apart all filthiness and superfluity of naughtiness, and receive with meekness the engrafted word, which is able to save your souls.
22 But be ye doers of the word, and not hearers only, deceiving your own selves.

Matthew 8:16-17
16 When the even was come, they brought unto him many that were possessed with devils: and he cast out the spirits with his word, and healed all that were sick:
17 That it might be fulfilled which was spoken by Esaias the prophet, saying, Himself took our infirmities, and bare our sicknesses.

1 Peter 2:24
Who his own self bare our sins in his own body on the tree, that we, being dead to sins, should live unto righteousness: by whose stripes ye were healed.

Quote it out loud to the sickness, and watch Satan run from you in terror! It may take a little while because Satan does not give up so easy sometimes! But you keep on saying it! He will go! Get up, move what was immovable while ago! Rise and be healed! Act as if God's Word were true! Hallelujah! The Lord really laid this on my heart for this month!) Some one really needs to hear this! If you know of someone that can use this please do not hesitate to copy and paste and send it on! Be sure and follow up with us, and stay with us! I believe you are going to do it! No matter what!!! .....do not give up!

"Don't ever let religious tradition rob you of the inheritance Jesus left for you! Healing, forgiveness, deliverance, peace joy, and prosperity belong to you according to God's Word! These are part and parcel with your salvation!

Thirty

Religion vs. The Word

Welcome to the National Atheist's Holiday - April 1!

We began a study last month on this subject of religion versus the Word and I would love to continue it here today!

Oh! How the religious leaders fought, and still fight, against this mighty baptism in the Holy Spirit! They even go so far as to suggest that speaking in tongues is of the devil! I repeat! You cannot go along with many religious leaders, or their traditions!

According to a Word Driven Life (Not religious tradition) you can still be baptized in the Holy Ghost! (This is contrary to many denominational teachings! But let's stick with the Word of God that has brought us "safe this far!"

The Bible says, *"In the mouth of two or three witnesses shall everything be established!"* I will give you 6 witnesses from the Word of God concerning the baptism in the Holy Ghost! John the Baptist says in Matthew 3.

1. *Matthew 3:11*

I indeed baptize you with water unto repentance. but

he that cometh after me is mightier than I, whose shoes I am not worthy to bear: he shall baptize you with the Holy Ghost, and with fire:

2. *Mark 1:8*

   I indeed have baptized you with water: but he shall baptize you with the Holy Ghost.

3. *Luke 3:16*

   John answered, saying unto them all, I indeed baptize you with water; but one mightier than I cometh, the latchet of whose shoes I am not worthy to unloose: he shall baptize you with the Holy Ghost and with fire:

4. *John 1:29-33*

   29 The next day John seeth Jesus coming unto him, and saith, Behold the Lamb of God, which taketh away the sin of the world.
   30 This is he of whom I said, After me cometh a man which is preferred before me: for he was before me.
   31 And I knew him not: but that he should be made manifest to Israel, therefore am I come baptizing with water.
   32 And John bare record, saying, I saw the Spirit descending from heaven like a dove, and it abode upon him.
   33 And I knew him not: but He (God!) that sent me to baptize with water, the same said unto me, Upon whom thou shalt see the Spirit descending, and remaining on him, the same is he which baptizeth with the Holy Ghost.
   (This is John quoting God!) So God mentions it!

O.K. But did Jesus mention The baptism in the Holy Ghost?

In *Acts 1* (Referring to Jesus speaking to His disciples after His resurrection.)

> *Acts 1:3-5*
> *3 To whom also he shewed himself alive after his passion by many infallible proofs, being seen of them forty days, and speaking of the things pertaining to the kingdom of God:*
> *4 And, being assembled together with them, commanded them that they should not depart from Jerusalem, but wait for the promise of the Father, which, saith he, ye have heard of me.*
> *5 For John truly baptized with water; but ye shall be baptized with the Holy Ghost not many days hence.*

These are the 6 witnesses that mention the baptism in the Holy Ghost! Matthew, Mark, Luke, John, and Jesus and God Himself!

Do we need any further confirmation of this subject? I think not!

What will happen when you are baptized in the Holy Ghost?

> *Acts 1:8*
> *But ye shall receive power, after that the Holy Ghost is come upon you: and ye shall be witnesses unto me both in Jerusalem, and in all Judaea, and in Samaria, and unto the uttermost part of the earth.*

What is the power for?

To be witnesses (Powerful, loving, and supernatural witnesses) to Jesus' death, burial, and resurrection to this lost and dying world! Supernatural witnesses! Glory!

Oh! Again I say "Oh! How the religious leaders fight against this baptism in the Holy Spirit! I repeat! You cannot go along with many religious leaders, or their traditions!

> *Acts 2:1-4*
> *1 And when the day of Pentecost was fully come, they were all with one accord in one place.*
> *2 And suddenly there came a sound from heaven as of a rushing mighty wind, and it filled all the house where they were sitting.*
> *3 And there appeared unto them cloven tongues like as of fire, and it sat upon each of them.*
> *4 And they were all filled with the Holy Ghost, and began to speak with other tongues, as the Spirit gave them utterance.* (120 were present and filled!)

This was the first day of the Church Jesus started! The Birthday of the Church! Now! I believe God is intelligent! He probably started the kind He wanted! They were all baptized in the Holy Spirit as prophesied by John the Baptist and Jesus, and God the Father!

Yes! This is still for the Church today! No matter what "They" say!

The book of Acts is to be a pattern for the Church of Jesus Christ until His return!

Thirty-One

Somebody Bigger Than You and I!

Who made the mountains,
Who made the trees,
Who made the rivers,
Flow to the seas,
And Who brings the rain when the earth is dry?
Somebody bigger than you and I!

These words are from a song made popular by Elvis Presley.

I would like to take that thought and expound on it.

In *Genesis 1* the Bible says that In the beginning God created the heavens and the earth! (No small feat!)

The Word for *God* there was translated from the compound word *Elohim*. (Pronounced *EL-OHEEM*)

The first part of that name (EL) means, (and it is extremely hard to say this with paper and ink) **The God of total, absolute, majestic, unlimited power!!**

The last part of that name is -OHIM. You cannot say that

without it being plural. Meaning Father, Son, and Holy Ghost. The meaning of the whole word when joined together means The God of total, absolute, majestic, unlimited power. three in One, Those Who create!

Nothing is impossible to Him!

He is bigger than sickness and disease!
He is bigger than oppression, and depression!
He is bigger than worry and fear!
He is bigger than poverty and lack!
He is bigger than marriage problems, and rebellious kids!

These verses come from Isaiah

> *Isaiah 40:10-12, 21, 25-26, 28-31*
> *10 Behold, the Lord GOD will come with strong hand, and his arm shall rule for him: behold, his reward is with him, and his work before him.*
> *11 He shall feed his flock like a shepherd: he shall gather the lambs with his arm, and carry them in his bosom, and shall gently lead those that are with young.*
> *12 Who hath measured the waters in the hollow of his hand, and meted out heaven with the span, and comprehended the dust of the earth in a measure, and weighed the mountains in scales, and the hills in a balance?*
>
> *21 Have ye not known? have ye not heard? hath it not been told you from the beginning? have ye not understood from the foundations of the earth?*
>
> *25 To whom then will ye liken me, or shall I be equal?*

saith the Holy One.
26 Lift up your eyes on high, and behold who hath created these things, that bringeth out their host by number: he calleth them all by names by the greatness of his might, for that He is strong in power; not one faileth.

(What can you say in comparison to His Greatness, His bigness if you will!)

28 Hast thou not known? hast thou not heard, that the everlasting God, the LORD, the Creator of the ends of the earth, fainteth not, neither is weary? there is no searching of his understanding.
29 He giveth power to the faint; and to them that have no might he increaseth strength.
30 Even the youths shall faint and be weary, and the young men shall utterly fall:
31 But they that wait upon the LORD shall renew their strength; they shall mount up with wings as eagles; they shall run, and not be weary; and they shall walk, and not faint.

So we see that our God is a mighty God! ***And He has said He will never leave you nor forsake you! Through Him we are more than conquerors!***

We can do all things through Him Who strengthens us!

If God be for us who can be against us! The Lord is on my side, I will not fear!

The Lord my God in the midst of me is MIGHTY!

On top of all this, He loves me so much He gave His only begotten Son, so that I could have everlasting LIFE! (And Many other benefits!)

> *Psalms 103:1-5*
> *1 Bless the LORD, O my soul: and all that is within me, bless his holy name.*
> *2 Bless the LORD, O my soul, and forget not all his benefits:*
> *3 Who forgiveth all thine iniquities; who healeth all thy diseases;*
> *4 Who redeemeth thy life from destruction; who crowneth thee with lovingkindness and tender mercies;*
> *5 Who satisfieth thy mouth with good things; so that thy youth is renewed like the eagle's.*

Hallelujah! He is big enough to do what He says!

REJOICE!!! He is your God if you have received Jesus as Lord and Savior!

Greater is He that is in you than he who is in this World!

Rise up! Shout it! You win!!

Thirty-Two

Taking Another Look

You have heard the old saying, *"Kicking over sacred cows"*?

Well I have a new twist to that saying! *"Giving the boot to religious 'Bull' in our lives!"*

I have been thinking about this for some time.

Is it ever proper when praying the prayer of faith to pray Thy will be done Lord, not mine?

Just delete the word "IF" and it is OK!

Well this is distinctively different from praying If it be Thy will. You see if you know the will of God as spelled out in the Word, it is perfectly acceptable to pray Thy will be done!

Because according to the Bible in:

Isaiah 55:8-9
8 For my thoughts are not your thoughts, neither are your ways my ways, saith the LORD.
9 <u>For as the heavens are higher than the earth, so are my ways higher than your ways, and my thoughts than</u>

<u>your thoughts.</u>

So it stands to reason that His will is far greater for our blessings than most of us can comprehend!

Ephesians 5:17
Wherefore be ye not unwise, but understanding what the will of the Lord is.

But it would be wise to remember this found in:
Ephesians 3:20-21
20 Now unto him that is able to do exceeding abundantly above all that we ask or think, according to the power that worketh in us,
21 Unto him be glory in the church by Christ Jesus throughout all ages, world without end. Amen.

Also remembering the fact that Jesus Himself prayed in Luke.

Luke 11:1-4
1 And it came to pass, that, as he was praying in a certain place, when he ceased, one of his disciples said unto him, Lord, teach us to pray, as John also taught his disciples.
2 And he said unto them, When ye pray, say, Our Father which art in heaven, Hallowed be thy name. Thy kingdom come. ***<u>Thy will be done, as in heaven, so in earth.</u>***
3 Give us day by day our daily bread.
4 And forgive us our sins; for we also forgive every one that is indebted to us. And lead us not into temptation; but deliver us from evil.

Notice Jesus said, *"Thy will be done on earth, as it is in heaven!"* Now, is there any sickness in heaven? Any lack or poverty? Any depression, or anxiety there? Fear or doubt?

Jesus brought the will of God to earth as in heaven as He healed the sick, cast out devils, raised the (young) dead, and set the captives free, and fed the hungry!

> *Luke 4:16-21*
> *16 And he came to Nazareth , where he had been brought up: and, as his custom was, he went into the synagogue on the sabbath day, and stood up for to read.*
> *17 And there was delivered unto him the book of the prophet Esaias . And when he had opened the book, he found the place where it was written,*
> *18 The Spirit of the Lord is upon me, because he hath anointed me to preach the gospel to the poor; he hath sent me to heal the brokenhearted, to preach deliverance to the captives, and recovering of sight to the blind, to set at liberty them that are bruised,*
> *19 To preach the acceptable year of the Lord.*
> *20 And he closed the book, and he gave it again to the minister, and sat down. And the eyes of all them that were in the synagogue were fastened on him.*
> *21 And he began to say unto them, This day is this scripture fulfilled in your ears!*

What is that? That is the will of God for the earth!!!

God asked me one day *"What's wrong with my will being done in your life and circumstances?"* Folks you might not be asking for His highest and best! He may have a better blessings in store for you than you can think or imagine!

The church world has always come at this as being humble, and negative. Such as God I want to live, but if You want me to die instead, just go ahead and kill me!

If you want me to suffer some more let Your will be done as You know what's best for me!

I would like to have a nice car, but I will be satisfied with an old clunker if that is Your will?

**He is not the God Who is barely enough,
He is the God that is MORE THAN ENOUGH!**

Noooo ! That's not it! *His will is for you to prosper and be in health even as your soul prospers!* So let's take it from God's point of view! We just may not be asking for enough! I mean we may be asking for 100 dollars and He has in mind 100,000 dollars! Do you see what I am trying to get across here!

His will for you is far greater than we, in our false humility, and small thinking, are willing to ask for!

We think "If I can just get enough to survive, I'll be happy!"

He is thinking *"Christ became poor, that you might be made RICH!"* He is thinking *"He that spared not His only Son but gave Him up for us all, how shall He not with Him give us all things?"*

So praying "Thy will be done, and not mine could give you a boost in the blessing you are seeking!

"Well you might as well say AMEN! It's all so anyhow, as Brother Hagin used to say!

Think about it!!

Thirty-Three

Thanksgiving

We have so much to be thankful for!

It's almost unbelievable, but its almost Thanksgiving again! We are so blessed as Americans because our forefathers set aside a day to give thanks to the One and Only, Almighty, Compassionate God and Father of our Lord Jesus Christ! We, as Americans, and as born again Christians, have so much to be thankful for! Just look at the Word of God in:

> *John 3:16*
> *"For God so loved the world that He gave His only begotten Son, that whosoever believes in Him shall not perish, but have everlasting life!"*

Hallelujah! We could spend every moment of every day giving God thanks and it still would not be enough!

> *Hebrews 13:15*
> *"By Him (Jesus) therefore let us offer the sacrifice of praise to God continually, that is the fruit of our lips, giving thanks to His Name!"*

May I take the Liberty of paraphrasing that verse for you?

> Because of what Jesus has already accomplished for us through His death, burial, and resurrection, let us offer the sacrifice of praise to God, that is the fruit of our lips, giving thanks to His Name!

Katherine Kuhlman said it like this "In the light of what Jesus has already accomplished through His death, burial and resurrection, what's left but praise! (And thanksgiving!)

Let's ask ourselves the question "What has Jesus done?"

> *Isaiah 53:5*
> *"He was wounded for our transgressions, He was bruised for our iniquities, the chastisement of our peace was upon Him, and by His stripes we are healed!*

Not only that but He was "*...manifested to destroy the works of the devil." (1 John 3:8)*

Do we owe Him a debt of gratitude or what? We need to develop an attitude of gratitude! According to the Word of God we are told to come into God's presence with Thanksgiving *(Psalms 100)*. Not grumbling and complaining, but with sincere, heartfelt, thanksgiving! Really if you want to know the truth about it, this is a major part of living by faith!

> *Hebrews 11:6*
> *"But without faith it is impossible to please Him!"*

Now bearing this in mind let's turn to:

> *Psalms 69:30-31a*
> *30 I will praise the name of God with a song,* (your will is involved) *and I will magnify Him with thanksgiving*
> *31 This also shall please the Lord!"*

Wait a minute! I thought you couldn't please the Lord without faith? So it must be that Thanksgiving and praise must be Faith in action, because it pleases the Lord!!

Thank God We Have Victory

> *Colossians 1:12*
> *Giving thanks unto the Father who has made us able to be partakers of the inheritance of the saints in light!*

Thank God we have an inheritance in Christ! According to *Romans 8:17* we born again ones are *heirs of God and joint -heirs with Jesus Christ!* All that Jesus has inherited, we have inherited through Him! Glory to God! !

> *Corinthians 15:57*
> *"Thanks be unto God who gives us the Victory through our Lord Jesus Christ!*

Thank God we have victory over sin, sickness, poverty, devils, demons, fear, and depression through what Jesus has done! Actually **we have victory over all the works of the devil in Jesus Name!**

Luke 10:19
Behold I give unto YOU power to tread on serpents and scorpions (Symbols of demonic power)

God through the death burial and resurrection of the Lord Jesus Christ has provided *exceeding abundantly above all that we could ask or think! (Ephesians 3:20)* Everything a human being could imagine (that is good and lovely) is already provided! All we need to do is begin to thank Him for His provision, walk in the light of His Word, and we will begin to know in reality the fullness of that provision!! In fact we can give thanks before we see the answer with our natural eyes, because we know God has promised and that He cannot lie!

Shout unto God with a voice of triumph!

Thank God!!

Thirty-Four

Meditation in God's Word

Hebrews 11:6
But without faith it is impossible to please him: for he that cometh to God must believe that he is, and that he is a rewarder of them that diligently seek him.

All of God's people would love to have more faith!

1 John 5:4
"For whatsoever is born of God overcometh the world: and this is the victory that overcometh the world, even our faith."

Most of us Christians understand the need for faith. It is true there is only one way that faith comes!

Romans 10:17
"So then faith cometh by hearing, and hearing by the word of God."

We need to examine this a bit further. If faith came by just hearing the Word we would all be faith giants. Most of us have heard more good solid Word than all generation behind is!

Jesus said, ***"He that hath faith to hear....let him hear."*** We know that everyone listening in that particular crowd had those two funny little things hanging on the side of their heads called ears. So He must have ben referring to something else other than just hearing with those physical ears. Of course that was part of it. But the Bible says that real faith "Is of the heart" Not referring to that physical blood pump in our chests!

> *Mark 11:23*
> *"For verily I say unto you, That whosoever shall say unto this mountain, Be thou removed, and be thou cast into the sea; and shall not doubt in his heart, but shall believe that those things which he saith shall come to pass; he shall have whatsoever he saith.*

I have found this out by years of experience in my own life and the lives of others that if the Word is not coming out of your heart; a person can say it 3000 times a day and it will not work for you!

Now! The problem is to get the life giving Word of God down from your ears and head, into your heart!

There are so many people that casually read the Word, memorize the Word, Quote chapters of the Word, but don't have a clue as to how to use the Word in everyday life. How do I know? Look at all the misery, pain, sicknesses, depression, poverty and yes even premature deaths in the Body of Christ today. They can quote the Word per Word, and they wonder why it is not working for them. Many times it is the way they are hearing the Word.

Most of Christianity today just read the Bible to make their quota for the day! Some proudly say "Well I read my 5 chapters today" Well that's good but what did you learn? What did the Word have to say? Most cannot answer the question. I have found that in most cases that there is a missing ingredient. They just sort of skim over the Scriptures but get very little spiritual nutrients from it!

> *Jeremiah 15:16*
> *"Thy words were found, and I did eat them; and thy word was unto me the joy and rejoicing of mine heart: for I am called by thy name, O Lord God of hosts."*

What did He mean he ATE them"?

Joshua 1:8 Explains it a little further.

> *"This book of the law shall not depart out of thy mouth; but thou shalt meditate therein day and night, that thou mayest observe to do according to all that is written therein: for then thou shalt make thy way prosperous, and then thou shalt have good success."*

Note: Who is going to *"make thy way prosperous"*? You or God?

YOU!!

Who is going to get you *"Good success?"*

YOU!!

We have all heard of the saying part, but few have taken the

"Meditating day and night" part seriously! Sometime hours and days go by without giving the word a thought!

This is just as big a part of having good success as the saying and doing is! Meditating on God's Word is like eating something until you get all the nourishment out of it possible. We are told all the way through the Bible the benefits of meditating on the Word. This is part of the Work mentioned for entering into rest!

I would rather read one verse a day and think about it, roll it over and over in my thinking, muttering what I have read throughout the day and get it....than read 5 chapters and retain none of it! Meditate on it until it becomes LIFE in you! When you eat natural food it actually becomes life and strength to you. So does "eating" meditating on the Word feed your Spirit man. It takes a little time and effort to chew properly!

Meditate on God's Word until you can "see" (imagine) yourself as God says you are in His Word! See yourself a new creation instead of that old thing you used to be! Righteous instead of beaten down with sin! Healed instead of sick and dying. More than a conqueror, a devil destroyer not a wimp. Prosperous not broke and lacking!

The Lord spoke to me and actually spoke this to me while I was in bed reading these things *"USE YOUR IMAGINATION"*

Worry is nothing more that imagining negative things! You can worry while you work, or play, or whatever without any effort!! Why can't we turn it around and imagine good things?

"Finally, brethren, whatsoever things are true, whatsoever things are honest, whatsoever things are just, whatsoever things are pure, whatsoever things are lovely, whatsoever things are of good report; if there be any virtue, and if there be any praise, think (Imagine) on these things.

Thirty-Five

The Awakening

Billye Brim (with whom I have been aquainted with for many years) was at a prayer meeting at her Prayer Mountain Lodge. They were praying about, and interceding for, the upcoming elections when the Lord gave her a Word about the 2008 Presidential election.

The Lord said that there is only one hope for America, and it is not a man or a political party!

He said, *"The only hope for America is an awakening to God!"*

Miss Brim went on to say that she got to thinking about it, and said "If the best man in the country got elected, it would make no difference without America waking up to God!"

She said they spent some time in real weeping and repentance, and began praying again but for an awakening to God!

A Pastor friend and his wife, and my wife Bonnie and I, had the pleasure of attending Billye's meeting in Branson this past October, and were greatly moved by the call to prayer for this awakening to take place!!

So when we got home, the Pastor and I, and our wives, were compelled by the Holy Ghost to start a prayer meeting to specifically pray about this demonic attack against our great nation. I call it "Prayer with an attitude!" Make no mistake about it, satan is pulling out all the stops, and is trying to take America down!

Psalms 11:3
If the foundations be destroyed, what can the righteous do?
(I have more information about this on this website)

The very Christian foundation, and fabric that made this country great are under an all out attack by satan and his minions. Many people and politicians are being duped, and playing into satan's hands!

Our Holy Spirit inspired Constitution is being challenged by our politically correct oriented politicians. They say it's too old fashioned! It must be brought up to date!

But I say Truth is always Truth! No matter how long it in existance!

Romans 1:22-25
22 Professing themselves to be wise, they became fools,
23 And changed the glory of the uncorruptible God into an image made like to corruptible man, and to birds, and fourfooted beasts, and creeping things.
24 Wherefore God also gave them up to uncleanness through the lusts of their own hearts, to dishonour their own bodies between themselves:
25 Who changed the truth of God into a lie, and wor-

shipped and served the creature more than the Creator, who is blessed for ever. Amen.

Why is this being done? Because we as a nation are sending the light of the glorious Gospel to nations in darkness! To people without God, strangers from the Covenant, to a lost and an undone, hopeless people!

We (The Church) allowed satan (by staying indifferent and prayerless) to take prayer out of schools, the 10 commandments out of public places, to put pornography on our airwaves and the internet, to cause the abortion of 45 million precious babies, and may I say casinos on every block almost, and it is time for the Church to rise up out of complacency, and apathy and take her rightful place!

Well, you may say "We already know this, ...but what is the answer to all this?

GOD!

It is time for the Church to get on its knees and begin to pray! All the while remembering

James 5:16b
"The effectual fervent prayer of a righteous man availeth much."

The Amplifed Version says it like this:
The earnest (heartfelt, continued) prayer of a righteous man makes tremendous power available [dynamic in its working].

John Wesley made this statement "It seems that God is limited as to what He can do for humanity unless someone asks Him to!"

James 4:2
"You have not because you ask not!"

Many in the Church have entered into a place of slothfulness! Self centeredness! Even many of our ministers have watched almost helplessly, as though nothing can be done!

But I have news, Church !

We have been given charge and authority over this earth by God; and we had better stand up and fight!

Can I prove this Scripturally? Yes I Can!

Ephesians 6:10-18
10 Finally, my brethren, be strong in the Lord, and in the power of His might.
11 Put on the whole armour of God, that ye may be able to stand against the wiles of the devil.
12 For we wrestle not against flesh and blood, but against principalities, against powers, against the rulers of the darkness of this world, against spiritual wickedness in high places.
13 Wherefore take unto you the whole armour of God, that ye may be able to withstand in the evil day, and having done all, to stand.
14 Stand therefore, having your loins girt about with truth, and having on the breastplate of righteousness;

15 And your feet shod with the preparation of the gospel of peace;
16 Above all, taking the shield of faith, wherewith ye shall be able to quench all the fiery darts of the wicked.
17 And take the helmet of salvation, and the sword of the Spirit, which is the word of God:
(Notice all this is PRAYER ARMOR!)
18 Praying always with all prayer and supplication in the Spirit, and watching thereunto with all perseverance and supplication for all saints;

(Notice we are not at war with men)

For we wrestle not against flesh and blood, but against principalities, against powers, against the rulers of the darkness of this world, against spiritual wickedness in high places.

Luke 10:19 (this is Jesus talking to all Christians!)
"Behold, I give unto you power to tread on serpents and scorpions, and over all the power of the enemy: and nothing shall by any means hurt you."

God's power has been given to the Church over all devils and demons!

Let's take that power and pray and take this country back!

So, with urgency, I call on all Christians everywhere to join us in real Holy Ghost lead prayer for America !!

Thirty-Six

The Blood is Sufficient

When God was leading His people Israel out of a 40 year Egyptian bondage He gave them specific instructions as to what they must do if they expected to survive. Not only to just survive, but if they were to depart victoriously, they must obey these instructions.

The firstborn of every household of the Egyptians would die if not covered by this blood of a lamb, and so would the first born of the Israelites if they failed at their task.

Their Instructions:

Exodus 12:22
And ye shall take a bunch of hyssop, and dip it in the blood that is in the bason, and strike the lintel and the two side posts with the blood that is in the bason; and none of you shall go out at the door of his house until the morning.

God placed much value on this blood of a lamb (which was just a type and shadow of the blood of the real Lamb of God ...Jesus)

Exodus 12:23
For the LORD will pass through to smite the Egyptians; and when he seeth the blood upon the lintel, and on the two side posts, the LORD will pass over the door, and will not suffer the destroyer to come in unto your houses to smite you.

In the morning when they awoke it was to the scene of destruction! The firstborn of the Egyptians was indeed dead, from the lowliest servant to the son of the Pharoah of Egypt. BUT!!! The Blood was sufficient! The destroyer had to honor the Blood!! The people of Israel were spared.

Glory To God!!

Hebrews 9:22
And almost all things are by the law purged with blood; and without shedding of blood is no remission. (of sins)

You must remember this lamb used in Egypt was just a symbol (type) of the Lamb of God that was to come!

John 1:29
The next day John seeth Jesus coming unto him, and saith, Behold the Lamb of God, which taketh away the sin of the world.

How was He to accomplish this wondrous feat?

Jesus the Lamb of God must shed His blood for the sins of the whole world! From Adam's fall to the end of the Age.

Matthew 26:28
For this is my blood of the New Testament, which is shed for many for the remission of sins. (Of the whole World)

When Jesus was beaten beyond recognition, then went to the Cross, had nails driven through His precious hands and feet, and finally pierced in His side by a cruel Roman spear, the pure sinless Blood of God was shed for all mankind!

You see God made a covenant with Abraham in the 17th chapter of Genesis.

Genesis 17:1-4
1 And when Abram was ninety years old and nine, the LORD appeared to Abram, and said unto him, I am the Almighty God; walk before me, and be thou perfect.
2 And I will make my covenant between me and thee, and will multiply thee exceedingly.
3 And Abram fell on his face: and God talked with him, saying,
4 As for me, behold, my covenant is with thee, and thou shalt be a father of many nations.

Genesis 17:10
This is my covenant, which ye shall keep, between me and you and thy seed after thee; Every man child among you shall be circumcised.

Abraham's covenant with God was a blood covenant. Abraham shed his blood at the time of his circumcision, but in order that a blood covenant to be ratified it required blood to be shed by both parties involved. God gave a substitute for His blood over the years, the sacrificial lambs! When did God actually shed His blood? When God allowed His Son to come and die for the sins of the whole world!

> *John 3:16*
> *For God so loved the world, that he gave his only begotten Son, that whosoever believeth in him should not perish, but have everlasting life.*

Thank God! The Blood has been shed, the stripes have been laid, the nails have been driven!

> *Hebrews 9:11-14*
> *11 But Christ being come an high priest of good things to come, by a greater and more perfect tabernacle, not made with hands, that is to say, not of this building;*
> *12 Neither by the blood of goats and calves, but by his own blood he entered in once into the holy place, having obtained eternal redemption for us.*
> *13 For if the blood of bulls and of goats, and the ashes of an heifer sprinkling the unclean, sanctifieth to the purifying of the flesh:*
> *14 How much more shall the blood of Christ, who through the eternal Spirit offered himself without spot to God, purge your conscience from dead works to serve the living God.*

The Blood is sufficient!

Now the destroyer *goes about as a roaring lion seeking whom he may devour!*

Sickness, poverty, depression, anxiety, fear, failure, doubt, thoughts and feelings of Hopelessness……suicide, giving up are Satan saying "The blood was not sufficient…..

Every attack of Satan is saying "The blood was not sufficient……..

All self-righteousness, religious ideas, trying to make it into heaven under your own steam and good works. Feelings of guilt over past sins is Satan saying …. The Blood was not sufficient…….

How are we to answer this deceiver?

> *Revelation 12:11*
> *And they overcame him by the blood of the Lamb, and by the word of their testimony; and they loved not their lives unto the death.*

Thank God!

I have news for the devil! (He knows it already!)

The Blood is sufficient today!

Use the Blood today to chase off Satan and his lies!

Shout in the face of all contradictory evidence! (Pain! Weakness! Fear! Poverty! Even death itself!

Satan! I am redeemed by the Blood of the Lamb!!

Plead the Blood!

He will flee from you and will not be able to come through your camp (home) either!

Thirty-Seven

The Bully

A little boy about 7 years old, named Timmy, came home one day and was scuffed up and had a brand new black eye.

The boy tried his best to sneak in, but his dad saw him, as he came through the front door.

The dad asked Timmy what had happened to him.

Oh!" He replied with shame in his voice The bully beat me up today.

"Uh huh! And how long has this been going on"? asked the dad.

"Bout 2 weeks" he answered.

"Well son, who is this bully?"

"He is the kid who lives just down the street. His name is Billy Bob."

"Well son I have seen that boy, and isn't he in your grade at school?"

"Yes." He replied.

"Why son, He is no bigger than you! Why do you put up with it?"

"Cause..... he's the bully dad!"

"Why don't you tell that boy to leave you alone or else?"

"I am afraid daddy! I don't want to make him mad!"

"Boy! You have my name! A part of me is in you!"

"No! the dad says.This is not going to do!"

"I want you to tell him you are going to whip him!

"In fact we are going down to his house right now, and challenge him to a fight in the gymnasium tomorrow!"

"No daddy! No Daddy!" The boy cried! "Nobody whips the bully! He will knock my head off!"

"No!" the dad replied! "You are gonna whip him! I will be there to see that it is a fair fight! You will both have boxing gloves on, and there will be a referee!"

So they both march down to the bully's house, the little boy being dragged by his dad is screaming all the way. "No! Daddy!"

Dad knocks on the door, and the bully himself answers.

The dad asks, "Have you been beating up my boy on the way to school? he asked the kid.

"Yep!" Was the reply.

"Are you gonna do it any more?"

"First thing in the morning!" answered the bully, as he glares at Timmy and smashed one hand into the other making a frightful sound.

The dad then issued the challenge!

They were to meet at the appointed time after school and have a showdown.

(Meanwhile, Timmy is devastated! Fear gripped him from the top of his head to the soles of his feet!)

The next day dragged by so agonizingly slow for little Timmy! He couldn't eat! He didn't sleep all night!

He just knows full well how this all is going to turn out. And it ain't good!!

The last bell rang dismissing school, and the time has come.

The boy thought about running but. where could he go?

Daddy picks Timmy up for the drive to the gym!

A small crowd had gathered fearing the worst for little Timmy.

The gloves are put on, and they climb into the ring. The dreaded moment has arrived!

Timmy is shaking, and quaking in his shoes!

They meet in the middle of the ring.

The referee explains the rules. The bell rings! And the fight is on!

The bully came running across the ring like a roaring lion!

Timmy held up his hands to block the fearfully anticipated first punch!

Pow! And Timmy is staggered!

A few more punches and he is on the ground!

"Daddy!" He screams! "Help me!" As he lies on the floor!

The dad says "No! Get up! You have my name! A part of me is in you! Whip him! You can do it! Don't be afraid!"

Well, the bell rang signifying the end of round one, and Timmys head is swirling. He staggers to his corner, not believing dad is putting him through all this!

The 2nd round bell rings and it's on again! The same thing happens for 3 rounds!

Timmy finds himself lying on the floor again about halfway through the fourth round!

Timmy begins to think like this! "Well! It looks like daddy is not going to help me! And I have had all this beating I am going to take!

I'm not putting up with this anymore!

Anger flashes across his face! He jumps to his feet! Eyes flashing! Determind! Eye of the Tiger!

(Right here is a good place for you to hear in your mind the theme song from Rocky!)

He grits his teeth and wades into the bully! Fists flying, and finding their mark! Bam! Pow!

When Timmy comes to himself the bully is laying on the ground crying, with stark fear in his eyes!

It is over! The battle is over! And Timmy has won!

The crowd is cheering! Pride and joy consumes Timmy as he goes to his dad! His dad is also filled with pride and joy! "I told you son!"

"You can whip him! He is no match for you! He will not

bother you again, or he will face the same beating you gave him this time!! You know how you whipped him this time .....so you can do it again if you need to!!"

Now my dear Brother and sister in Christ! Satan is threatening! He is attacking with sickness, depression, fear, poverty, and discouragement! Anxiety grips you! Circumstances point to complete defeat! Feelings cry out "There is no way!"

But you have been born again! Born of God! A child of the KING! You have the Name of Jesus! You have been filled with the Holy Ghost! You have been filled with God Himself! You have His WORD! You have the Blood of Jesus! You have on the full armor of God! Get Up!

God the Father (Daddy) is cheering you on!

He is saying "Get up! You can whip him. Get up off the mat! I've done all I am going to do about the devil! Now it is up to you! You may be down, but you are not out! Get up and whip him! You have my name, my blood, the Holy Ghost, my WORD, a part of me is in you!

Fight the good fight of faith!

> *James 4:7*
> *"Resist the devil and he will run from you as in terror!"*

Now! Rise up, and just DO IT! You are a winner! Not a whiner! You cannot be defeated and you will not quit! Rise Up!

Isaiah 60:1-3
1 The Spirit of the Lord God is upon me; because the Lord hath anointed me to preach good tidings unto the meek; he hath sent me to bind up the brokenhearted, to proclaim liberty to the captives, and the opening of the prison to them that are bound;
2 To proclaim the acceptable year of the Lord, and the day of vengeance of our God; to comfort all that mourn;
3 To appoint unto them that mourn in Zion, to give unto them beauty for ashes, the oil of joy for mourning, the garment of praise for the spirit of heaviness; that they might be called trees of righteousness, the planting of the Lord, that he might be glorified.)

Glory to God!!

▪ (Credit to whom credit is due! I got the idea for this story from the late Pastor John Osteen, I just added my own characters and story line)

Thirty-Eight

The Church Final Addition

Matthew 16:18
....I will build my church...and the gates of hell will not prevail against it.

In previous newsletters we discovered that Jesus started the church with supernatural demonstrations of the Spirit and Power!

Just check *Acts 2:1-4* to see the actual birth of the Church Jesus started!

We left off last month with the thought that the Church was to be a supernaturally empowered Church filled with the Holy Ghost. That is the Church (People who are born again) was to be filled with resurrection power to demonstrate to the world that Jesus had risen from the dead. To prove with infallible proof that "He's not here! He has arisen." Just as the angel had said!

How?

Notice how the Church began praying!

Acts 4:29
"Grant unto us that we may speak your word boldly! And that signs and wonders may be done in the name of your Holy Child Jesus!"

Notice the way the "early Church" prayed!

IS THIS REALLY REAL?

Now we must come to the realization that the Holy Ghost resides in the believer today!

Paul asks some born again believers "What! Don't you know that your bodies are the temples of the Holy Ghost? They were filled, but they did not know it! They did not perceive it! They did not grasp it! Paul is trying to get it across to them! What about the Church today? Could this have been written for us as well? Would Paul ask the same question today?

1 John 4:4
"You are of God little children, and have over come then because Greater is He (The Holy Ghost) that is in you, than he (the devil) that is in the world!

<u>The greater One lives in us! He is greater than the devil, or sickness, or poverty, or any problem you may be facing today!</u>

Is it really true? We are the temples of the Holy Ghost? The same Spirit that raised Jesus from the dead is now actually residing in us? And He has lost none of His power!!

SELAH!

(Pause and calmly think of that!)

Think of it! Let me say it again! According to *Romans 8:11* the same Spirit that raised Jesus from the grave, out of hell itself, out of Satan's grasp, is now living in us! **And He will make alive our mortal body!**

This is not at the last resurrection, but "mortal body" means the body you are living in right now! Hallelujah! I think this is a good place to just shout a little bit! Maybe even dance a little!

I often say to a congregation while I am preaching "What if the whole Bible was true?" They look at me stunned for even suggesting that it may not be true! I do this to get people's attention! If the whole Bible is true, and it is, then the Holy Ghost has come to take up residence in every believer!

To make you a superman, or superwoman, or super-teenager, or? Praise God!

God is waiting for the revelation knowledge of this to come to the "modern day church." Waiting for us to grasp the fullness of this Biblical truth! Waiting for us to rise up and take our place as the Church Jesus started, and is still perpetuating today!

Now what is He in you for?

> *Acts 1:8*
> *"But you shall receive power, after that the Holy Ghost has come upon you, and you shall be witnesses to me.....*

to the uttermost parts of the earth! (Wherever you may live or travel to!)

Thank God! Jesus did not leave us here to be the slaves of a merciless devil! Not as wimps to fall for his every trick! But to ***"Rule and reign as kings in this earth!"*** He intended for us to "Occupy until I come." "Occupy" means to rule over, as when a country is taken over after a war, as we occupied Japan after WW 2.

John 1:12
12 To as many as received Him, to them He gave the power to become the son's of God, even to them who believe on His name!
13 Which were born, not of the blood, nor of the will of the flesh, nor of the will of man, BUT OF GOD!

Again think of it!
We are the children of the MOST HIGH GOD!

No wonder Jesus said in *John 14:12 "Verily I say to you, he that believes on me, the works that I do, shall he do also!"* GLORY TO GOD!

Notice He did not say that the "early disciples, or the early Church would do these works! He said "He that believes!" That's you and me!

That's why Paul could say in
1 Corinthians 2:4-5
4 "And my speech and my preaching was not with entic-

> *ing words of mans wisdom, but in demonstrations of the Spirit and of power,*
> *5 That your faith should not stand in the wisdom of men, but in the power of God!"*

Now! How do we match up to the early believers? Are we doing "The works" He did?

Let's get to doing the Works that were promised to us! Let's rise up in resurrection power and make Jesus proud of us! Let's show Him He did not waste His time by coming and going to the cross! Let's take this supernatural power to our lost and dying world! He is waiting for us to take our place!

Let's just DO IT!

Thirty-Nine

The Church (Part 1)

Matthew 16:13-18
13 When Jesus came into the coasts of Caesarea Phillipi, He asked His disciples, saying, Whom do men say that I the Son of Man am?
14 And they said Some say that you are John the Baptist; some Elijah, and others Jeremiah, or one of the Prophets
15 He said to them But who do you say I am?
16 And Simon Peter answered and said You are the Christ, the Son of the living God.
17 And Jesus said You are blessed Simon Bar-Barjona: for flesh and blood has not revealed this to you, but my Father which is in heaven.
18 And I say to you that you are Peter, and upon this rock <u>I will build my Church; and the gates of hell shall not prevail against it.</u>

Jesus said; "I will build my church"

Jesus tells us here that He is going to build His Church! Contrary to many folks belief, Jesus is not telling Peter the Church is going to be built upon him! Jesus is saying I will build My Church upon what you said You are the Christ, the

Son of the Living God!

Compare this to

Romans 10:9

If you (anyone) will confess with your mouth that Jesus is Lord, and believe in your heart that God raised Him from the dead, you will be saved. (Born again)

Jesus said to a very religious man in

John 3:7

Marvel not that I said You must be born again!

There is only one way to get into the Church that Jesus started You must be born again.

Notice that Jesus did not say I will build my churches, plural! Church is in the singular!

Do not misunderstand me though! People from any denomination who get born again belong to His Church. But on the other hand, a person can belong to any church and still not receive Christ as their personal Savior, and still not belong to Christ's Church!

Jesus went as far as to say unless you are born again you will not see the Kingdom of God.

When Jesus said Church, He was not saying there will be an Early Church and a latter Church The only difference between the Early Church and the Latter Church is that the Early church came earlier! But there was to be no fundamental difference between the two!

I hear all the time from many that (healing, miracles, baptism in the Holy Ghost, Tongues, etc...) was only for the early Church, and all that stopped when the disciples died! The only thing that stopped when the disciples died was the disciples!

I always ask for what Chapter and verse is their opinion based on?

There is nothing in the Bible that says these things will disappear from the Church!

On the contrary, there are many indications that these things were to continue throughout the ages! (I challenge anyone to prove me wrong with Scripture!)

You have a decision to make.

So to be a member of the Church that Jesus began, you must be born again. Well, someone might say, they do not teach that at my church. Well then you have a decision to make! Belong to yours, or belong to Christ's.

Many say from different "religions" that they are going to the same place (heaven) they are just on another road like Buddha, or Mohammed or some other invented god.

Jesus said in

John 14:6

I am the Way the Truth, and the life. No one can come

to the Father except through Me.

So if you are on any other road to heaven other than Jesus, you are on a dead end road! To put it another way Your way or the Highway His way is the Highway!!

You shall be baptized in the Holy Ghost

Jesus gave instructions to the people that would be members of His Church after His resurrection in the book of *Acts Chapter 1.*

Acts 1:3-5, 8
3 (The disciples) *to whom He showed Himself alive by many infallible proofs, being seen of them 40 days and speaking of many things pertaining to the kingdom of God.*
4 And being assembled together with them, commanded them that they should not depart from Jerusalem, but wait for the promise of the Father?
5 For John truly baptized with water, but you shall be baptized in the Holy Ghost not many days hence!

8 But you shall receive power after that the Holy Ghost has come upon you, and you shall be witnesses to me in all the world.

Forty

The Church (Part 2)

Last month we left off with *Acts 1:8.*

> *You shall receive power after that the Holy Ghost has come upon you, and you shall be witnesses unto me to the uttermost part of the Earth.*

Witnesses

What kind of witnesses? Powerful witnesses!

That means the Church (the Church He builds) will be a powerful, world changing, body of believers who will demonstrate the goodness of God to this lost and dying world!

There is no mention of a weak emaciated Church at the mercy of a merciless devil. Filled with all kinds of sorrow and grief or poor, poverty stricken, sick, fearful people. Begging for the Lord to come back and rescue them from this world! No mention of bingo, or church sponsored dances! No, a thousand times no!

Traditions of Men

Traditions of men brought all these things to the Church!

Things such as "There are no more miracles, or healings, or speaking in tongues. We no longer need such things!"

What does Jesus say to these traditions?

> *Making the Word of God of none effect through your tradition and many such like things you do! (Mark 7:1-13)*

This is not the Church Jesus envisioned when He came to earth to build His Church! *(Matthew 16:18)* To give His life, and shed His blood for!

You will notice on the day of Pentecost, the birthday of His Church, that it all began with a powerful demonstration of the Spirit and power!

> *Acts 2:1-4*
> *1 And when the day of Pentecost had fully come they were all with one accord in one place.*
> *2 And suddenly there came a sound from heaven as of a rushing mighty wind , and it filled all the house where they were sitting.*
> *3 And there appeared unto them cloven tongues like as of fire, and it sat upon each of them* (There were 120 of them, not just 12)
> 4 *And they were all filled with the Holy Ghost, and began to speak with other tongues as the Spirit gave them utterance.*

Glory to the Almighty God! A supernatural beginning!

God is Intelligent

This was the beginning of the Church that Jesus started! And if you will give God credit for being intelligent, this must have been the kind of Church He wanted! A powerful Church!

The book of Acts is a pattern for the Church until Christ returns!

These folks on the day of Pentecost were to be witnesses (to prove with infallible proofs to the known world) the resurrection of Jesus! The Church was a powerful entity on the earth, resulting in the salvation of thousands! 3,000 got saved after hearing and seeing the things that went on that day, and hearing Peters powerful sermon!

God Demonstrates His Goodness

Acts 3:1- 10
1 Now Peter and John went up together into the temple at the hour of prayer.
2 And a certain man lame from his mothers womb was carried, whom they laid daily at the gate of the temple which is called Beautiful, to ask alms of them who entered into the temple;
3 Who seeing Peter and John about to go into the temple asked an alms.
4 And Peter fastening his eyes upon him with John, said "Look on us".
5 And he gave heed unto them expecting to receive something from them.

6 Then Peter said "Silver and gold have I none, but such as I have I give to you. In the Name of Jesus Christ of Nazareth rise up and walk.
7 And he took him by the right hand and lifted him up; and immediately his foot and ankle bones received strength.
8 And he leaping up stood, and walked, and entered in with them into the temple, walking, and leaping, and praising God.
9 And all the people saw him walking and praising God.
10 And they knew that it was the man they had seen daily at the gate begging alms. And they were filled with wonder and amazement. **Hallelujah!**

This resulted in a great crowd gathering and offered Peter the chance to preach the Gospel to them. Another 5,000 were saved that day!

What a contrast between the Church then and the Church now!

Forty-One

The Church (Part 3)

Matthew 16:18b
I will build my church, and the gates of hell will not prevail against it!

We left off speaking about the Church Jesus started!

We decided that God was intelligent so He must have started the kind of Church He wanted!

In The Beginning

We noticed that the Church was born in the book of *Acts Chapter 2:1*.

The Church started with supernatural demonstrations of the Spirit and Power!

A mighty rushing wind, tongues of fire, speaking in tongues in many unlearned languages.

These supernatural happenings drew a crowd of many people.

Peter and John got a man born crippled healed, and Peter preached a sermon about Jesus, and 3000 people got saved. Healing, and supernatural happenings, are the dinner bell to the Gospel!

We are comparing the Church that Jesus started in the book of Acts to the modern day Church.

<u>The book of Acts is a pattern of the Church to all generations!</u>

The Church's Great Commission

Let's look at the Great Commission that Jesus left the Church just before His ascension into heaven.

> *Mark 16:15-20.*
> *15 Go ye into all the world and preach the Gospel* (Good news) *to every creature.*
> *16 He that believes and is baptized shall be saved* (Born Again) *but he that does not believe shall be damned.* (Not only live a cursed life but in the end go to hell)

Many churches teach this as the Great Commission, but this is only part of it!

> *17 And* (This means He is not finished speaking yet!) *these signs shall follow them that believe.* (Not just you 11 disciples) *In My name they shall cast out devils, they shall speak with new tongues,*
> *18 they shall take up serpents, and if they drink any deadly thing it shall not hurt them. They shall lay hands*

on the sick, and they shall recover.
19 So then after the Lord had spoken to them, He was re-
ceived up into heaven, and sat on the right hand of God.
20 And they went forth, and preached everywhere, the
Lord working with them, and confirming the Word with
signs following! Praise the Lord.

The Church was to be a bunch that was supernaturally equipped, supernaturally empowered! Ambassadors to this lost and dying world!

We were never meant to be a groaning, defeated, sick, fearful bunch of people praying for the Lord to come quickly to take us out of this devil-infested world! Noooooo! Never!

Jesus meant for the Church to take His place!

Have you ever read *John 20:21?*

> *Verily verily I say to you, he that believes on me , the works that I do shall they to also, and greater works than these shall they do because I go to the Father.*

This staggers the imagination when taken at face value, and believed! Remember God cannot lie! People can, but God never!

How about *1 John 4:17b*

> *...because as He (Jesus) is so are we in this world.*

What about *Matthew 5:14*

> *You are the light of the world! Let your light so shine before men that they may see your good works and glorify*

your Father in heaven!

What are the good works that are referred to here?

His works, and greater.

Ephesians 2:10
We are God's workmanship, created in Christ Jesus unto good works, which God had before ordained that we should walk in them.

Paul writes in *1 Cor. 6:19* to born again, Spirit filled believers and asks them this question.

What?

What! Don't you know that your body is the temple of the Holy Ghost which is in you, which you have of God, and you are not your own? For you are bought with a price. (The Blood of Jesus) Therefore glorify God in your body, and in your spirit, which are God's! (Notice! Your body has been bought as well as your spirit!)

Praise God if you receive Jesus as Lord and Savior, your body is the temple of the Holy Ghost! If you receive the Baptism in the Holy Ghost you receive the power that raised Jesus from the dead! *(Romans 8:11)* That is resurrection power!

Is it possible the people Paul was writing had that power dwelling in them, and did not know it? Or not taking advantage of it!

Could it be that many (most) in the Church today could be in the same position! Filled with supernatural power, and not know what they have? Could this account for the difference in the Early Church and the Church today?

Forty-Two
The Foundation

To paraphrase a familiar phrase:

"Friends, Oklahomans, and Country men,
lend me your ears!"

Since this is a month in which we celebrate our independence, I would love to interject some of my own thoughts on the direction we are headed!

I have wanted to write this newsletter for a long time and it seems right to me, and to the Holy Ghost, that this is the opportune time!

There is much going in our nation that I, and probably millions of others, would like to address! I cannot possibly get all that I would like to say in one newsletter, but I will try with God's help to hit some of the highlights!

Isaiah 60:1-3
1 Arise, shine; for thy light is come, and the glory of the LORD is risen upon thee.
2 For, behold, the darkness shall cover the earth, and

gross darkness the people: but the LORD shall arise upon thee, and his glory shall be seen upon thee.
3 And the Gentiles shall come to thy light, and kings to the brightness of thy rising.

Arise, and shine here means to me:

Christians! Stand up and be counted! Speak up! Shout it from the rooftops!

It is a time to speak out for what is right in the great United States of America!

The Bible speaks here of a great darkness covering the earth, and overtaking the people.

Well, we can plainly see that happening in our nation. From the decisions of our courts, to much public opinion, which is being shaped by our (for the most part) godless media in the U.S.A., we are changing.

I was born in 1944, and I have seen many changes in our country. Some good and some not so good! I am sorry to say that since the early 1960s much of it has been not so good! I very often say while preaching the Gospel that if you were raised in the same era I was raised in, and went to sleep in 1961 and did not wake up until today, you would think you were in a foreign country when you observed many of the changes in America!

Over 50 million (at this time) babies slaughtered under the guise of women having the say-so over their own bodies.

And the same government who passed this law, has passed another one that says children must wear seat belts! Even if it is about their own bodies! Where is common sense? It seems the inmates are running the asylum.

People need to understand the founding principles of our nation. Anyone who says that this nation was not founded on Christian principles and morals is either deceived or lying! Of course I am limiting this to anyone smart enough to read. It would take volumes to quote our founding father's belief in God, and references to God and His Son Jesus Christ. But I will quote a few if you will indulge me.

Our very beginning, with the Mayflower compact was filled with references to God. And there is no doubt as to what God they are referring to, as they almost always refer to Jesus in their letters, and speeches!

THE MAYFLOWER COMPACT

In the name of God, Amen. We whose names are under-written, the loyal subjects of our dread sovereign Lord, King James, by the grace of God, of Great Britain, France, and Ireland King, Defender of the Faith, etc.

Having undertaken, for the glory of God, and advancement of the Christian faith, and honor of our King and Country, a voyage to plant the first colony in the northern parts of Virginia, do by these presents solemnly and mutually, in the presence of God, and one of another, covenant and combine ourselves together into a civil body

> *politic, for our better ordering and preservation and furtherance of the ends aforesaid; and by virtue hereof to enact, constitute, and frame such just and equal laws, ordinances, acts, constitutions and offices, from time to time, as shall be thought most meet and convenient for the general good of the Colony, unto which we promise all due submission and obedience. In witness whereof we have hereunder subscribed our names at Cape Cod, the eleventh of November [New Style, November 21], in the year of the reign of our sovereign lord, King James, of England, France, and Ireland, the eighteenth, and of Scotland the fifty-fourth. Anno Dom. 1620.*

Can there be any intelligent reason to challenge this historical document? Many act as if this document was a forgery!

From the ending of our 4th President's (James Madison) First Inaugural Address come these Words:

> *But the source to which I look or the aids which alone can supply my deficiencies is in the well-tried intelligence and virtue of my fellow-citizens, and in the counsels of those representing them in the other departments associated in the care of the national interests. In these my confidence will under every difficulty be best placed, next to that which we have all been encouraged to feel in the guardianship and guidance of that Almighty Being whose power regulates the destiny of nations, whose blessings have been so conspicuously dispensed to this rising Republic, and to whom we are bound to address our devout gratitude for the past, as well as our fervent*

supplications and best hopes for the future.

I can only pray that these historical remarks will be taught again in our public school systems. No more rewriting history.

They took prayer, and the 10 Commandments, out of our publicly funded schools, and what did they replace them with? Metal detectors! I know they are proud. As it stands today, in my opinion, the National Educational Association should be abolished, and replaced with honest God fearing people! This goes for the ACLU as well! (The ACLU was started by card carrying communists) Check it out yourselves!

I have a book I would like to recommend concerning this subject! *"None Dare Call It Education"* by John Stormer.

Someone please tell me how the writings (The Ten Commandments, and other Scriptural quotations) on most of our government's capitol buildings got there. Did they just all of a sudden appear, or were they carved by our predecessors? Please check out this link for more on this subject! http://www.rickmcknightministries.com/modules.php?name=EyeOpener

Do you suppose they knew the Constitution of the United States when they did that? How do you suppose they were allowed to do that, especially under today's misinterpretation of the Constitution?

I could quote from George Washington (who is referred to as the Father of our Nation) Abraham Lincoln, and other great statesmen of the past who mentioned God in their public speeches. But, as I said earlier, it would take volumes to quote all that was said about God Almighty by these founders of our nation.

I guess they would be included under that Christian Right Wing Conspiracy!

I read this statement in a grammar school Principal's office.

"In case of nuclear attack, the law against prayer in schools will be temporarily lifted!"

Sort of says it all doesn't it?

Please pray for our nation!

Perfect? No! Blessed by God? Yes!

Still (as of today) the greatest nation on earth!

I would like to conclude by saying this!

This Nation is great not because of our government, but because of our Great and Mighty God.

God Bless America!

Forty-Three

The High Life

In *Genesis 1: 1-25* God had just created the Earth and everything on it. Plus the moon, the sun, and the stars.

What a mighty God we serve!

What was all this for? Why did He do it?

The Plan

On the sixth day God created the reason for creation! Man!

Notice Adam was created just in time for the day of rest! All the work was accomplished!

Then God says to the Son and the Holy Ghost in:

> *Genesis 1:26*
> *And God said, Let us make man in our image, after our likeness: and let them have dominion over the fish of the sea, and over the fowl of the air, and over the cattle, and over all the earth, and over every creeping thing that creepeth upon the earth.*

Psalms 115:16
The heaven, even the heavens, are the LORD's: but the earth hath he given to the children of men.

Everything He created He gave into the hands of man! He did it for man!

So I can truthfully say, man was created to live **the HIGH LIFE!**

No sickness, no poverty or lack, no death, no sin! God had already provided all their needs before they got there! Man was to be happy, healthy, and blessed!

The Plan Disrupted

Genesis 3 - The Fall of Man

Genesis 3:1-7
1 Now the serpent was more crafty than any of the wild animals the LORD God had made. He said to the woman, "Did God really say, 'You must not eat from any tree in the garden'?"
2 The woman said to the serpent, "We may eat fruit from the trees in the garden,
3 but God did say, 'You must not eat fruit from the tree that is in the middle of the garden, and you must not touch it, or you will die.' "
4 "You will not surely die," the serpent said to the woman.
5 "For God knows that when you eat of it your eyes will be opened, and you will be like God, knowing good and evil."
6 When the woman saw that the fruit of the tree was

good for food and pleasing to the eye, and also desirable for gaining wisdom, she took some and ate it. She also gave some to her husband, who was with her, and he ate it.
7 Then the eyes of both of them were opened, and they realized they were naked; so they sewed fig leaves together and made coverings for themselves.

When Adam and Eve partook of the fruit in disobedience to God's command, they fell into a lower (Satan's) kingdom.

They were created in a high Kingdom of the blessings of God. When they committed sin (disobedience to God's Word) they fell under a curse into a lower kingdom God's original plan for them to live the high life was thwarted.

God Has Another Plan

Genesis 3:14
So the LORD God said to the serpent, "Because you have done this, "Cursed are you above all the livestock and all the wild animals! You will crawl on your belly and you will eat dust all the days of your life.

First God curses the devil.

Genesis 3:15
And I will put enmity between you and the woman,and between your offspring and hers; he will crush your head, and you will strike his heel."

Then God starts speaking of a Redeemer when He mentions her offspring. The King James Version says between your seed and her seed.

That seed of woman spoken of here, is Jesus!

Several thousand years later Jesus is born of a virgin in a manger.

Why has He come?

8 He who does what is sinful is of the devil, because the devil has been sinning from the beginning. The reason the Son of God appeared was to destroy the devil's work.

What is the devil's work? -- Sin, Sickness, and poverty!

He came to set mankind free from the works of the devil that came with the fall!

Jesus came to give the Life of God back to mankind!

Jesus speaks of His mission compared to Satans in:

John 10:10
The thief (Satan) comes only to steal and kill and destroy;
I have come that they may have life, and have it to the full.

The Life that Jesus speaks of here is the Life that Adam had before the fall! It was the very Life of God! In the Greek it is the Word '*Zoe*'.

John 14:6
Jesus answered, "I am the way and the truth and the life.

I like to call it **the High Life!**

Jesus demonstrates, in His life and ministry, what a man filled with God's life can do!

How Do I Get This High Life?

John 3:1-3
1 Now there was a man of the Pharisees named Nicodemus, a member of the Jewish ruling council.
2 He came to Jesus at night and said, "Rabbi, we know you are a teacher who has come from God. For no one could perform the miraculous signs you are doing if God were not with him."
3 In reply Jesus declared, "I tell you the truth, no one can see the kingdom of God unless he is born again."

John 3:7
You should not be surprised at my saying, 'You must be born again.'

The instant a person gets born again **they receive The High Life!**

2 Corinthians 5:17
Therefore, if anyone is in Christ, he is a new creation; the old has gone, the new has come!

Now the journey begins to learn to live in this High Life!

God designed it to be a glorious life of peace, joy, health, and prosperity! <u>With authority over all</u> that comes to steal, kill, and destroy! (Satan)

Forty-Four

The Light!

Satan is referred to very often as the Prince of Darkness!

Did you ever notice that if a person is ill they almost always feel worse when the sun goes down? When the light goes out! Fever increases, pain increases, fear and anxiety increases. Most alcohol, and drugs are consumed after dark. (I could go on and on!)

How about criminal activity? Most of it is done in the darkness of night. Most sin is committed in darkness, or at least where the criminal, or sinner, hopes they won't be seen or caught!

Why?

Because all that stuff is of the devil! Satan likes to remain in the darkness, hidden, and skulking around where he hopes not to be identified! To go undetected!

(This is why it is a God idea to have a curfew before midnight for your kids!)

All you have to do is shine a light on an intruder at night and he, most likely, will scurry away like a bug so as to avoid incarceration, or worse, avoid being killed by squashing!

When Jesus appeared on earth it was into a world of darkness. Particularly spiritual darkness. But He came as a light!

John 1:1-5
1 In the beginning was the Word, and the Word was with God, and the Word was God.
2 The same was in the beginning with God.
3 All things were made by him; and without him was not any thing made that was made.
4 In him was life; and the life was the light of men.
5 And the light shineth in darkness; and the darkness comprehended it not.

The light came to earth to shine the light on all that darkness had perpetrated on mankind! He came not only to reveal all that was hidden in the darkness, but to do something about the Prince of Darkness, and his hidden agenda.

1 John 3:8b
For this purpose the Son of God was manifested, that he might destroy the works of the devil.

How did He destroy Satan's works?

Matthew 4:23
And Jesus went about all Galilee, teaching in their synagogues, and preaching the gospel of the kingdom, and healing all manner of sickness and all manner of disease among the people.

We can ascertain what Jesus was preaching by the results!

Healing!

..and healing all manner of sickness and all manner of disease among the people.

(He was destroying Satan's works by healing the sick!)

Romans 10:17
"Faith comes by hearing and hearing by the word of God!"

<u>So He must have been preaching on healing!</u>

What was Jesus doing? He was shining His light on the old religious ideas that were probably believed in His time such as "God will make you sick to teach you a lesson!" "After all, God is behind everything, good or bad." ...or "Healing stopped with Abraham". He was bringing to light where sickness really came from! Unmasking the thief!

John 10:10
The thief cometh not, but for to steal, and to kill, and to destroy: I am come that they might have life, and that they might have it more abundantly.

He was saying that Satan is like a burglar, or a thief, that works undercover of darkness, to steal all that you hold dear! *"The light came to the darkness, and the darkness "comprehended it not"*.... or *"the darkness could not do anything about it!"* **Hallelujah!**

Any one remember seeing some of the old war movies where the Americans were huddled in the darkness in foxholes, and their job was to hold the enemy? They could not see the enemy? All of a sudden a flare was sent up, and lit up the hillsides that were filled with advancing enemy soldiers! What happened? Machine guns began to roar, rifles began to shoot, hand grenades came from everywhere!

The enemy had to be discovered before he could be dealt with!

Well! **I want you to know the Light has come!** And the enemy unveiled! Satan and his bag of tricks has been revealed! Now it is up to the children of light to commence firing!

Lock and load!

Colossians 1:12-14
12 Giving thanks unto the Father, which hath made us meet to be partakers of the inheritance of the saints in light: Thank God we are not fooled by the darkness anymore! We are children of the Light!
13 Who hath delivered us from the power of darkness, and hath translated us into the kingdom of his dear Son:
14 In whom we have redemption through his blood, even the forgiveness of sins:

When we got born again we stepped out of the "power (authority) of darkness" into the Kingdom of His Dear Son, which is the Kingdom of light!

The Light!

Matthew 5:14-15
14 Ye are the light of the world. A city that is set on an hill cannot be hid.
15 Neither do men light a candle, and put it under a bushel, but on a candlestick; and it giveth light unto all that are in the house.

Now, as born again Spirit-filled believers we are to let our light shine into this world of darkness, even to those in our own household! To reveal to this lost and dying world that Satan is behind sickness and disease, and that Jesus came to set them free!

How do we turn the light on? By words and actions that reveal the truth to people! We tell them what the Word says, then lay hands on them after they know the Truth! Darkness (All sickness, disease, pain, poverty, fear, depression) must bow it's knee!

This little light of mine! I'm gonna let it shine!

Praise God!

Forty-Five

The Nature of Faith

A friend of mine was speaking to their congregation when she heard these Words from the Lord! *"My people think they are living by faith, when actually they are living on a low grade of hope!"*

Many think that faith is for anyone but themselves! When our Bro. John Osteen was still living on earth he found himself complaining and murmering about some things going on in their life. Pastor Osteen had a congregation of several thousand. Dodie, his wife, was listening to this tirade when she said a simple truth! "John", she said, You need to go read some of your books!"

As I think about it we could all use this advice! We need to be practicing what we preach!

Many, even of our ministers, need to return to our roots taught by men such as Kenneth E. Hagin, T.L. Osborn, Fred Price, Charles Capps and EW Kenyon!

Many lay-Christians have forgotten the simplicity of faith, such as you can have what you say! Thousands of Christians think they must go through rigorous and many mental excercises, worry, and strain, to acheive real faith!

They have forgotten that real faith needs nothing more than "God said"!

Really there are only 2 platforms to stand on in faith! <u>Belief...or unbelief!</u> Either God meant what He said, or He didn't! His Word is either reliable or it is not!

Numbers 23:19 is always good to remember! *"God is not a man that He should lie!"*

If you truly believe that God is truthful you need not hesitate to act on God's Word! Regardless of not seeing any change in your situation!

If He says He loves you *(John 3:16)* ...don't argue with Him about it! If He says He will *supply all your needs (Phil. 4:19)* He will!

Faith is a decisive act! Stepping out on faith depending on nothing but God's Word! It is not stepping out on nothingness, but stepping out on the foundation of the World, which is God's Word!

Real faith ignores all symptoms that contradict God's Word! A prisoner was once petitioning the governor for a pardon. After many days he received a reply that said he was pardoned and could go free!

He went to the back of his cell and began to cry! Saying"Boy, I wish some one would get me out of here! The jailor said "Look here is your pardon! The prisoner responds "Yeah! I have read it, and I believe it, but I am still locked up! I sure wish I could get out of here!

Can't you see there would be no freedom for him if he refuses to act on the pardon!

All of mankind has been set free from sin and it's consequences, but millions refuse to believe and act on the pardon, and the new birth, given by God the Father. Many Christians remain bound by chains of sickness, fear, depression, etc... because they refuse to act on God's infallible Word!

Dear reader **you have been set free!** *John 8:31-32 and 36!*

'Start acting like your free, your not bound anymore! The chains of bondage have been broken, satan's lost the war!

The price has been paid in full, stand upright on your feet, and hold your head up high, and release words of faith!"

These words are taken from a song my Brother wrote called "Supernatural Life!" It is on one of my music CD'S and can be purchased on my website!

rickmcministries.com

Forty-Six

The Word

Psalms 11:3
"If the foundations be destroyed, what can the righteous do?"

This is a very foundational message, but we need to be continually reminded of these foundational truths as Born Again believers if we are going to experience God's best for our lives! No matter what you are facing, this truth will lead you to victory!

John 1:1
In the beginning was the Word, and the Word was with God, and the Word was God.

Now! If the Word (Bible Word!) ever was God, it is still God speaking to us today!

We need to give the Word the same place we would give Jesus if He were standing right in front of you speaking!

Matthew 4:4
But he answered and said, It is written, Man shall not

live by bread alone, but by every word that proceedeth out of the mouth of God.

Live by it! Live by it! Do it! Act on it! Practice it! Let it become a part of your being!

(I know! You have heard this before! But don't quit now!)

So when will we start to obey, or get back to, obeying, this in our lives! I will tell you this! The same Word that has brought you this far will work again!

I was preaching in Australia at Mt. Martha beach, (by Melbourne) when this incident occurred. I had been in the Ministry a number of years.

I was scheduled to speak at the evening meeting the next day. I was having a physical battle all night. My throat was sore, my sinus was clogged, I was running a fever, and I was going to speak on healing the next night.

I spent the entire night fussin with the devil. I would say in a weak WHISPERING voice No you don't devil! I will not have this!

Well! When dawn broke I was still ill! The Lord spoke to me and asked what I was doing.

(Of course He knew already!) I came to my defense and said I was rebuking the devil.

He then said for me to take my van and drive down to the beach. He wanted to speak with me!

I did as He said. He asked me again what I was trying to do. I told Him the same thing as before.

He then said to me in a bone rattling and thundering earth shattering voice, ***"When are you going to learn I am serious about My Word?"***

I was stunned for a moment and when I stopped shaking I said RIGHT NOW LORD! RIGHT NOW!

I then proceeded to tell Satan in a loud, thundering voice what I thought of him, and his sickness that he was trying to put, and keep, on me! Before I got back to the campgrounds I was well! *Psalms 105:20* had come to pass, along with *1 Peter 2:24! God watched over His Word and performed it! (Jeremiah 1:12)*

As born again children of Most High God the Word must be our final authority! The supreme court of the universe! **It is FINAL!**

Without acting on *St. John 3:1-8*, and *Romans 10:9-10*, or some similar Scriptures you and I would spend an eternity in hell! It is that serious!

But being Born again is only the start.. Not the finish! It is the start of a great journey that will not end until we pass away, or get raptured! Hallelujah!

His Word gives life and light, health and healing, prosperity, joy, and peace to us as believers!

It is a big mistake to just read it just once, or hear a sermon or two, then put our Bibles on the shelf!

Faith comes by hearing, and hearing, and hearing God's infallible Word! It is the Manufacturer's hand book! The Manufacturer (God) is smarter than you or me! *His ways are higher than our ways! (Isaiah 55:8)*

> *Jeremiah 15:16*
> *Thy words were found, and I did eat them; and thy word was unto me the joy and rejoicing of mine heart: for I am called by thy name, O LORD God of hosts.*

> *Hosea 4:6*
> *My people are destroyed for lack of knowledge: because thou hast rejected knowledge, I will also reject thee, that thou shalt be no priest to me: seeing thou hast forgotten the law of thy God, I will also forget thy children.*

Every Christian failure can be narrowed down to one of these 2 problems!

1. Either they do not know what God says, or
2. They do not obey what He says! (Reject His knowledge-Word)

What is the answer then?

1. Get into the Bible and find out what He says!
2. Obey what He says!

This will settle everything you face in life!

Marriage problems, children problems, money problems, depression, sorrow, sickness, anxiety, fear, worry, grief, ..all things are possible to God, if you will obey Him!

The same Word that has brought you this far will do it again and take you on through to absolute Victory! Get back into the Bible!

> *Joshua 1:8*
> *This book of the law shall not depart out of thy mouth; but thou shalt meditate therein day and night, that thou mayest observe to do according to all that is written therein: for then thou shalt make thy way prosperous, and then thou shalt have good success.*

(Complete Victory!)

GLORY!

Forty-Seven

There is No God???

I received an email the other day that told this story!

It seems there was this fellow was bringing a lawsuit against the government demanding that those in power should pass a law declaring a National Atheist's Day!

After hearing the man's argument the judge told the man that there already existed a day set aside for them!

Delighted the man asked What is that day?

The judge replied, "April First!"

(This is of course April Fools Day.)

This was sent as a joke, but there is a lot of truth to it as well. *Proverbs 14:1* says *The fool has said in his heart there is no God.*

I got to thinking along this line and thought about an incident that occurred many years ago in my life when the Lord spoke to me.

I was worried about a certain thing in my life instead of trusting Him for the victory.

This thing was like a dark cloud hanging over my head, and I was really in a stew!

The Lord asked what I was doing worrying about it!

Well I explained the problem to Him (as if He didn't know about it already!)

He then asked if I wanted to know what the real problem was.

I said, "Certainly!"

He said very gently "You are acting as if there were no God!" I want you to know I got over that worry very quickly! I did not realize that was exactly what I was doing!

I know that none of us as Christians would ever think of saying that out loud! But many times our actions (that speak louder than words) sometimes are shouting "There is no God!"

Jesus taught us that "We must be born again!"

2 Corinthians 5:17 says *"If any man be in Christ, they are a new creature!* In Ephesians it says we are to *"Put off the old man, and put on the new which is created after God in Righteousness and true Holiness!"*

In other words there will be a change in us that other people will see!

Jesus refers to us in *Matthew 5:14* as the "Light of the world!" And that we are to *"let our light shine before men that they may see our good works and glorify God!"* We are *"Ambassadors for Christ"* everywhere we go, and in everything we do and say is either saying there is a God, or "There is no God!"

Now it is plain to see that we are not expected to grow up overnight, but eventually there should be some changes in our lives!

I know one thing that changed in my life was a new vocabulary! It was almost an overnight change!

The friends that I hung out with gradually changed, along with what I drank! The places I used to go started to change! The music I listened to, and the shows I watched began changing. Why?

Because these things that I did were screaming "There is no God!" In fact every sin I commit is saying "There is no God!"

The Bible tells us how to grow as Christians!

1 Peter 2:22
As newborn babes, desire the sincere milk of the word, that ye may grow thereby:

We must feed our selves on God's Word daily!

Matthew 4:4
"But he answered and said, "It is written, Man shall not

> *live by bread alone, but by every word that proceedeth out of the mouth of God."*

Then learn to apply it to our daily lives! Live as though the Word was true! Cause it is!!

<u>The Word (Bible) is the Manufacturer's Hand Book!</u> It tells us how to live if we want to have, and live, the abundant life that Jesus spoke of in *John 10:10!*

The number one thing we need to learn is
To love the Lord our God!

Then "Love our neighbor as ourselves!"

These changes usually, (and should) show up in our family first! How to treat our wives or husbands and our children is clearly explained in Ephesians.

I have now been married to my lovely wife Bonnie for 46 years! We have 4 children.

Somebody asked what was the key to our long marriage! The answer is at least 3-fold!

- **First** - choose Jesus as Lord and Savior!

- **Second** - Put God's Word first place in your life!

- **Third** - Learn to treat your wife like a thoroughbred and you won't have to live with a nag!!

Choose God's Word over your "RIGHTS" and things will go well!

Well, some might say "She's not the raving beauty now she once was!

My answer: Look in the mirror Charlie!! Sideways!! Snap out of it!

Let's let our light shine before this world of darkness, so they may glorify our Father in Heaven!

Let's put actions to our Christianity! The world needs to see some change in us if we profess to be Christians!

You may have to find some new friends! New places to hang out! Improve your vocabulary to include some 5 letter words!! Learn clean jokes! Quit the booze! Stop taking the illegal drugs! But none of this will hurt you!!

But please, don't go on acting as if There were no God!

Forty-Eight

Victory Over Fear (Part 1)

Genesis 1:26
Then God said, "Let us make man in our image, in our likeness, and let them rule over the fish of the sea and the birds of the air, over the livestock, over all the earth, and over all the creatures that move along the ground."

Mankind was created to live in dominion over all the works of God's hands!

To be happy, joyful, healthy, and prosperous.

To "reign as a king in this life"!

But in *Genesis 3:1* he (Adam) sold out to satan and disobeyed God's instructions.

Up until this time Adam had walked with God in the cool of the day, without any sense of inferiority or guilt.

Now that they (Adam and Eve) had committed sin God comes looking for them to fellowship with them further.

Genesis 3:8
8 "Then the man and his wife heard the sound of the LORD God as he was walking in the garden in the cool of the day, and they hid from the LORD God among the trees of the garden.
9 But the LORD God called to the man, "Where are you?"
10 He answered, "I heard you in the garden, and I was afraid because I was naked; so I hid."

When they listened to the devil, and did what he said, the result was fear! They were afraid of God. This was the beginning of fear on the earth! And it came through Satan!

According to the word of God fear is a tormenting spirit! Fear is the exact opposite of faith. <u>Fear is "faith" in the devil.</u>

Someone has said that "On the wings of faith cometh God; On the wings of fear cometh the devil." And this is an accurate saying!

Let's look at what God says about fear

Isaiah 41:10
So do not fear, for I am with you; do not be dismayed, for I am your God. I will strengthen you and help you; I will uphold you with my righteous right hand.

Isaiah 54:4
Fear not; for thou shalt not be ashamed: neither be thou confounded; for thou shalt not be put to shame!!

Isaiah 54:8-17
8 In a little wrath I hid my face from thee for a moment; but with everlasting kindness will I have mercy on thee, saith the LORD thy Redeemer.
9 For this is as the waters of Noah unto me: for as I have sworn that the waters of Noah should no more go over the earth; so have I sworn that I would not be wroth with thee, nor rebuke thee.
10 For the mountains shall depart, and the hills be removed; but my kindness shall not depart from thee, neither shall the covenant of my peace be removed, saith the LORD that hath mercy on thee.
11 O thou afflicted, tossed with tempest, and not comforted, behold, I will lay thy stones with fair colours, and lay thy foundations with sapphires.
12 And I will make thy windows of agates, and thy gates of carbuncles, and all thy borders of pleasant stones.
13 And all thy children shall be taught of the LORD; and great shall be the peace of thy children.
14 In righteousness shalt thou be established: thou shalt be far from oppression; for thou shalt not fear: and from terror; for it shall not come near thee.
15 Behold, they shall surely gather together, but not by me: whosoever shall gather together against thee shall fall for thy sake.
16 Behold, I have created the smith that bloweth the coals in the fire, and that bringeth forth an instrument for his work; and I have created the waster to destroy.
17 No weapon that is formed against thee shall prosper; and every tongue that shall rise against thee in judgment thou shalt condemn. This is the heritage of the

servants of the LORD, and their righteousness is of me, saith the LORD.

2 Timothy 1:7
For God hath not given us the spirit of fear; but of power, and of love, and of a sound mind.

Hallelujah! God has told us not to be afraid! So rise up against every temptation, or thought, or imagination that would bring fear and stand against it! *Greater is He that is in you* than fear! **Speak to it! Tell it that it has no business in your life!**

You have been set free!

Forty-Nine

Victory Over Fear (Part 2)

We have discovered that **God created man to rule and reign with Him over the Earth.**

> *Genesis 1:26*
> *And God said, Let us make man in our image, after our likeness: and let them have dominion (authority) over the fish of the sea, and over the fowl of the air, and over the cattle, and over all the earth, and over every creeping thing that creepeth upon the earth.*

But both man and woman committed high treason by giving in to the devil's suggestions and disobeying God. Adam should have taken his dominion over the "creep" Satan and chased him out of the garden. But he stood passively by and allowed Satan to steal his wife!

When God came back looking for Adam, after the fall, Adam was afraid. This is the first mention of "fear" in the Scriptures. Notice that it was after Satan beguiled them. Sin will cause folks to be afraid of God and the judgement that follows. **Fear opens the door to Satan.**

Again, fear is the opposite of faith. It is faith, but in reverse. Faith in the negative. Faith works for good, and fear works for the evil.

According to the Scriptures, fear is a tormenting spirit.

The Lord spoke to me one day and said, *"Fear is to the mind, what cancer is to the physical body."*

I started to see the seriousness of this thing called fear, and the negative effect that it not only has on the mind, but also on the bodies of mankind.

I am going to quote a few Scriptures where God warns mankind **"Not to fear."**

1. *Genesis 15:1*
After these things the word of the LORD came unto Abram in a vision, saying, Fear not, Abram: I am thy shield, and thy exceeding great reward.

2. *Genesis 26:24*
And the LORD appeared unto him the same night, and said, I am the God of Abraham thy father: fear not, for I am with thee, and will bless thee, and multiply thy seed for my servant Abraham's sake.

3. *Genesis 46:3*
And he said, I am God, the God of thy father: fear not to go down into Egypt; for I will there make of thee a great nation:

4. *Exodus 14:13*

And Moses said unto the people, Fear ye not, stand still, and see the salvation of the LORD, which he will shew to you to day: for the Egyptians whom ye have seen to day, ye shall see them again no more for ever.

5. *Exodus 20:20*

And Moses said unto the people, Fear not: for God is come to prove you, and that his fearmay be before your faces, that ye sin not.

Well there are many more times that these words were spoken to mankind over the years and centuries. But for the sake of writing space I will give some examples of just a few more men who were told not to fear.

Joshua 1:1-2
1 Now after the death of Moses the servant of the LORD it came to pass, that the LORD spake unto Joshua the son of Nun, Moses' minister, saying,
2 Moses my servant is dead; now therefore arise, go over this Jordan, thou, and all this people, unto the land which I do give to them, even to the children of Israel.

Here we find God speaking to Joshua after Moses had died. Now why was God speaking to him? Because he was being tempted to walk in fear! (Well if you were about to take Moses' place pastoring around 2 million murmerers you would be a little nervous too!)

This is a drastic, so to speak, measure that God was taking, to physically speak to his future leader of Israel!

He goes on speaking to him;

(vs 3-9)
3 Every place that the sole of your foot shall tread upon, that have I given unto you, as I said unto Moses.
4 From the wilderness and this Lebanon even unto the great river, the river Euphrates, all the land of the Hittites, and unto the great sea toward the going down of the sun, shall be your coast.
5 There shall not any man be able to stand before thee all the days of thy life: as I was with Moses, so I will be with thee: I will not fail thee, nor forsake thee.
6 Be strong and of a good courage: for unto this people shalt thou divide for an inheritance the land, which I sware unto their fathers to give them.
7 Only be thou strong and very courageous, that thou mayest observe to do according to all the law, which Moses my servant commanded thee: turn not from it to the right hand or to the left, that thou mayest prosper withersoever thou goest.
8 This book of the law shall not depart out of thy mouth; but thou shalt meditate therein day and night, that thou mayest observe to do according to all that is written therein: for then thou shalt make thy way prosperous, and then thou shalt have good success.
9 Have not I commanded thee? Be strong and of a good courage; be not afraid, neither be thou dismayed: for the LORD thy God is with thee whithersoever thou goest.

Notice God commands him not to be afraid! Now why?

Because fear is of the devil! It makes communication with God very difficult! It takes good judgement away, and creates confusion! Fear causes one to tremble in the face of an enemy. God cannot have a fearful leader to lead his flock!

> *2 Timothy 1:7*
> *For God hath not given us the spirit of fear; but of power, and of love, and of a sound mind.*

Thank God when we were born again we were released from that tormenting devil of fear. But....he will still try to usurp the believer's authority by coming with fearful thoughts, and feelings of weakness, and discouragement. Making accusations against blood bought, and Spirit-filled believers.

What are we to do?

> *1 Peter 5:8-9*
> *8 Be sober, be vigilant; because your adversary the devil, as a roaring lion, walketh about, seeking whom he may devour:*
> *9 Whom resist stedfast in the faith, knowing that the same afflictions are accomplished in your brethren that are in the world.*

When fearful thoughts come resist them, recognizing that these thoughts are coming from Satan! Fear (Worry, stress, nervousness, hypertension, worry, anxiety) is considering what Satan says and then thinking these thoughts may be true!

No! Drive them out of your mind by speaking what God says!!

Shout at fear if necessary! It is your enemy! Take the Word of God (the sword of the Spirit) and start slicing fear up!

You are redeemed from it by the Blood of the Lamb!

Jesus was crucified, and has arisen from the dead so that you could be delivered from it!

Never give in to it!!!!

Fifty

Victory Over Fear (Part 3)

> *Isaiah 41:10 AMP*
> *Fear not [there is nothing to fear], for I am with you; do not look around you in terror and be dismayed, for I am your God. I will strengthen and harden you to difficulties, yes, I will help you; yes, I will hold you up and retain you with My [victorious] right hand of rightness and justice.*

We are admonished over and over again in Scripture not to fear! As I have said before fear is the opposite of faith! Fear works, as faith will, but it will bring the thing "not wanted". Job said about his malady *"That which I have greatly feared has come upon me."*

Fear attracts the negative, unwanted things of life, whereas faith attracts the things desired.

Let's look at what Isaiah has to say about this subject in

> *Isaiah 54:9-10, 13-14*
> *9 For this is like the days of Noah to Me; as I swore that the waters of Noah should no more go over the earth, so have*

I sworn that I will not be angry with you or rebuke you.
10 For though the mountains should depart and the hills be shaken or removed, yet My love and kindness shall not depart from you, nor shall My covenant of peace and completeness be removed, says the Lord, Who has compassion on you.

13 And all your [spiritual] children shall be disciples [taught by the Lord and obedient to His will], and great shall be the peace and undisturbed composure of your children.
14 You shall establish yourself in righteousness (rightness, in conformity with God's will and order): you shall be far from even the thought of oppression or destruction, for you shall not fear, and from terror, for it shall not come near you.

We are told here to establish ourselves in Righteousness!

If we do this look at the results! <u>We shall be far from oppression, for we shall not fear, and from terror will not come near us!</u>

(v 15)
Behold, they may gather together and stir up strife, but it is not from Me. Whoever stirs up strife against you shall fall and surrender to you.

Look at what the Bible calls fear and terror! **THEY** and **WHOEVER!** Fear and terror take on personalities! These are both demonic forces!

Look in *2 Timothy 1:7*

> *For God did not give us a spirit of timidity (of cowardice, of craven and cringing and fawning fear), but [He has given us a spirit] of power and of love and of calm and well-balanced mind and discipline and self-control.*

Fear here is referred to as a spirit! There is a fear that is definitely from the enemy! A spirit called "fear," and one called "terror."

> *(v 15 KJV)*
> *Behold, they (fear and terror) shall surely gather together, but not by me: whosoever shall gather together against thee shall fall for thy sake.*

Here we are told that fear and terror will come but God did not send them! But even when they do come they will fall for our sake!

> *(v 17 AMP)*
> *But no weapon that is formed against you shall prosper, and every tongue that shall rise against you in judgment you shall show to be in the wrong. This [peace, righteousness, security, triumph over opposition] is the heritage of the servants of the Lord [those in whom the ideal Servant of the Lord is reproduced]; this is the righ teousness or the vindication which they obtain from Me [this is that which I impart to them as their justification], says the Lord.*

It is up to you to show these spirits to be in the wrong! Every tongue means every voice, or thought that contradicts Gods

Word, you shall cast down! Speak "It is written" to fear! And it will run from you as in terror!

Refuse to be afraid any longer!

This is referring to *James 4:7*

Submit yourselves therefore to God. Resist the devil, and he will flee from you.

Notice here that fear and terror are also called weapons! But God promises ***"No weapon formed against us will prosper!"***

Because our Righteousness is of God *(2 Corinthians 5:21)* we can face these enemies and drive them out of our lives! Meditate on your righteousness!

Hallelujah! No more bondage!

Whom the Son sets free is FREE INDEED!

Fifty-One

Who was Born on Christmas Morn?

Here we are again in the month we celebrate the birth of our Lord and Savior Jesus Christ!

I think we all know that Jesus was really born during the fall season, but December the 25th was the day chosen by our forefathers as the day to recognize His birth.

I just want to write a personal note of appreciation to the Great Father God Who loved the World (Everyone in it) so much that He gave His only Son to live on earth, and for His miracle working, healing ministry to a lost and dying world!

He was born of a virgin.

He was born in a manger for there was no room for them at the Inn. He grew up under the Law of Moses and never broke one of them.

For what purpose has He come?

Luke 4:16-19
16 And he came to Nazareth, where he had been brought

up: and, as his custom was, he went into the synagogue
on the sabbath day, and stood up for to read.
17 And there was delivered unto him the book of the
prophet Esaias. And when he had opened the book, he
found the place where it was written,
18 The Spirit of the Lord is upon me, because he hath
anointed me to preach the gospel to the poor; he hath
sent me to heal the brokenhearted, to preach deliver-
ance to the captives, and recovering of sight to the blind,
to set at liberty them that are bruised,
19 To preach the acceptable year of the Lord.

Thank God He came to help people in every way possible!

(Not just to take people to heaven some day)

He fed the hungry, healed the sick, raised the dead, healed the mentally ill, cast out devils, calmed the sea, walked on the water, supplied fish to the fishermen, gave hope to the hopeless, and fulfilled the whole Law for us! (Among hundreds of other things!)

What did He get for all the wonderful things He did for mankind?

The religious people of the day had Him crucified.

But death itself could not hold Him down!

Remember the wonderful old song we sing at Easter?

Up from the grave He arose,
With a mighty triumph or' His foes,
He arose the Victor from the dark domain,
And He lives forever with His saints to reign!
He arose! He Arose! Hallelujah! Christ arose!

Jesus is no longer a babe in the manger!

He is the resurrected King of Kings, and Lord High Priest over the Church, He is the Alpha and Omega, and everything in between.

He is the Prince of Peace, the Everlasting Father, the wonderful Councilor, the Creator of the heavens and the earth!

He gives Life and breath to every creature on the earth.

He is the Savior of all mankind!

He is the way, the Truth, and the Life, He is the Mediator between man and God.

His Name is above all names, and *at His Name every knee shall bow, of beings in heaven beings on earth, and beings under the earth, and every tongue shall confess that JESUS Christ IS LORD to the Glory of God the Father!*

That's angels, men and demons must bow their knee, and confess that Jesus Christ is Lord! (And that is just the beginning of Who He is!!)

He is the soon coming King Who will live and reign forever!

Do you know Him?

Fifty-Two

You Can Have What You Say (Part 1)

Jesus, the Son of God, said in *Mark 11:23*

> *For verily I say unto you, That whosoever shall say unto this mountain, Be thou removed, and be thou cast into the sea; and shall not doubt in his heart, but shall believe that those things which he saith shall come to pass; he shall have whatsoever he saith.*

You must notice and take heed to what Jesus is saying here, and to whom He was speaking about!

> *He said "That whosoever shall say, and shall not doubt in his heart, but shall believe that those things which he saith shall come to pass; he shall have whatsoever he saith.*

I do not know how much clearer Jesus could have said it!

And He was absolutely talking to you if you are a "whosoever!"

What is Jesus talking about?

He is talking about the God kind of faith.

In order to really understand this verse of Scripture we must look at the previous verses in the

▸ In the 11th Chapter of Mark. Let's go back to some verses between 12 and 22!

> *12 And on the morrow, when they were come from Bethany, he was hungry:*
> *13 And seeing a fig tree afar off having leaves, he came, if haply he might find any thing thereon: and when he came to it, he found nothing but leaves; for the time of figs was not yet.*
> *14 And Jesus answered and said unto it, No man eat fruit of thee hereafter for ever. And his disciples heard it.*

> *19 And when even was come, he went out of the city.*
> *20 And in the morning, as they passed by, they saw the fig tree dried up from the roots.*
> *21 And Peter calling to remembrance saith unto him, Master, behold, the fig tree which thou cursedst is withered away.*
> *22 And Jesus answering saith unto them, Have faith in God.*

In these verses of scripture Jesus sees a fig tree from a distance and goes to it to find some figs to eat. (He is really going to teach His disciples an object lesson!)

There are no figs and Jesus speaks to the tree and says to it ***"No man shall eat from your fruit again forever!"***

What in the world is Jesus doing talking to a tree? Think about it!

Nothing seems to change about the tree immediately. No one says anything about it! I can imagine one of the disciples looking at the other and after rolling his eyes says "Whew! It sure has been hot out here today!"

They proceed into town to take care of some business. They then leave town, passing by the fig tree. No one notices it. The next morning they are heading back into town where they come to the fig tree again. Peter sees the tree and notices that it had *"dried up from the roots!"*

Peter draws attention to the fact of what Jesus did! But Jesus says *"Have faith in God!"* (Some translations say *"Have the God kind of faith"*)

He then goes on to explain what the God kind of faith consists of!

> *He said "That whosoever shall say, and shall not doubt in his heart, but shall believe that those things which he saith shall come to pass; he shall have whatsoever he saith.*

He is actually saying "No, Peter. It's not just what I can do! **Look what you can do!** This is the way the God kind of faith works! Believe in your heart, and say it with your mouth and you will (eventually) have what you say!"

This is a Kingdom law that cannot be denied! God said it, I believe it, and that settles it! Really God said it, and that settles it, if I believe it or not!

This law will work in the positive. (Saying what God says) or it will work in the negative because it is a spiritual law!

Just as surely as there are natural laws that always work (mathematics, gravity) There are spiritual laws that always work!

Jesus is basically saying "This is the way we operate in heaven, now I want you (Whosoever) to operate like this on earth!"

You are today a product of what you have been saying all your life! If you don't like your situation start saying something different!

What Am I To Say?

Start saying what God says!

About you, your health, your standing with Him, your finances, your mind, your emotions, everything!

For instance in, *2 Corinthians 5:17*

> *Therefore if any man be in Christ, he is a new creature: old things are passed away; behold, all things are become new.*

Start saying out loud *"I am a new creature in Christ!"* Old things are passed away!

What old things?

The old things of sickness, sin, fear, poverty, depression, and failure are passed away!

Hallelujah! Jesus said "***You can have what you say, if you will believe it in your heart and say it!***

I highly recommend a mini-book by Kenneth E. Hagin called "In Him"

In this book there are many Scriptures telling who you are since you came to Christ!

Meditate on the Word of God in this little book (The word *meditate* means to mutter, or to say) and your life will be changed forever!

If you cannot locate this book find Scriptures in the Bible that use the terms "In Him" "In Whom" "By Him" "through Him".

For instance *Ephesians 1:7*

> *In whom we have redemption through his blood, the forgiveness of sins, according to the riches of his grace;*

This is what you have "In Christ." Start saying it and it will become more real to you. Say it over, and over, and over!

> *He said "That whosoever shall say, and shall not doubt in his heart, but shall believe that those things which he saith shall come to pass; he shall have whatsoever he saith.*

Fifty-Three

You Can Have What You Say (Part 2)

We started this series by proving that by quoting Jesus in:

> *Mark 11:23*
> *For verily I say unto you, That whosoever shall say unto this mountain, Be thou removed, and be thou cast into the sea; and shall not doubt in his heart, but shall believe that those things which he saith shall come to pass; he shall have whatsoever he saith.*

Jesus was teaching them a spiritual law. He first spoke to the fig tree, while I am sure His disciples watched in quiet astonishment!

While passing by the fig tree the third time (once when He cursed it, again while leaving town, again while returning to the town) Peter called Jesus' attention to the cursed tree pointing out the tree was dried up from the roots! He said basically "Look at what you did to the fig tree Jesus!"

And Jesus said in essence *"No Peter! Look what you can do."*

Whosoever shall say...and not doubt in his heart...but shall

believe what he says shall come to pass, shall have whatsoever he says.

This is probably the most important teaching on faith that ever fell from the lips of the Master!

He was saying (if I may paraphrase) ***"This is the way we operate in heaven, now I want you to operate like this on earth!"***

What did He mean by that?

In order to understand this we should go back to the book of Genesis Chapter One!

How did God operate when He created the World?

Genesis 1:1-3
1 In the beginning God created the heaven and the earth.
2 And the earth was without form, and void; and darkness was upon the face of the deep. And the Spirit of God moved upon the face of the waters.
3 God said, "Let there be light: and there was light."

Here we find the Spirit moving on the face of the waters, but not doing anything else. He was waiting on something! What was He waiting for? He was waiting for God to speak! Why? So He could use the substance (Faith) of God's Words to create what God said!!

May I say God believed in His heart what He said would come to pass, and it did! He created all matter by speaking it into existence! What was the substance that came out of His mouth?

Hebrews 11:1
Now faith is the substance of things hoped for, the evidence of things not seen!

If you continue to read Genesis you will see the Words "God said" over and over! **This is the way God created what He wanted! By releasing His faith!** *He called those things which be not as though they were*, and they leaped into being! He spoke what He wanted and the Holy Spirit had some substance to work with to create!

Now think about that! Meditate on it for a while!

Jesus comes down from heaven and tells His human creation...

"Now you do the same thing!"

Whosoever shall say. Hallelujah! Do you see it?

He is giving us license to create our world with faith, believed in the heart, and spoken with the mouth. This gives the Holy Spirit something to work with for creating! He is waiting for the born again believer to say what he wants ..so He (The Holy Spirit) can create it! Many times this does not happen instantly, but what the believer says continually.

I must warn you though that today there are 2 forces waiting for the human to speak! Because the Bible says in...

Proverbs 18:21
Life and death are in the power of the tongue: and they that love it shall eat the fruit thereof.

Today both the Holy Spirit, and satan, are waiting for words to be spoken so they can use the substance called faith (or fear) to create what you say!

You see fear is faith in reverse, or faith in the negative. Words of fear will cause whatever is feared, and spoken, to come upon the individual. They believe it in their heart, and say it with their mouth, and they eventually have whatsoever they continually say!

Jesus did not say just the good things will be brought to pass! He said *"whatsoever he saith!"* (Good or bad)

Start Saying Something Different

Then according to what Jesus said, you are today a product of what you have been saying about yourself, about your health, about your mind and emotions, about your finances, about your circumstance, about your kids, etc.

So if you are not happy with your circumstances, Jesus would say Start changing what you are continually saying! Start saying what you want instead of what you see, think, or feel!

Again, start saying what God says about you, your mind and emotions, your health, and your children, and your finances! You will find that God's Word is true when it says in...

Jeremiah 1:12
"He watches over His word to perform it!"

But you must believe it in your heart, and say it for this to work!

Start today saying what you want in your life. Start saying what God says about you!

Find a verse of Scripture that applies to your situation and start speaking it!

Even if you don't believe it yet..... start saying it! The more you say it the more you believe it!

For instance the devil says to your mind "You can't start saying **"I can do all things through Christ who strengthens me!"** He may say "You're weak! You say back what God says "It is written, God is the strength and my song!"

Shout it! Say it BOLDLY! Whatever God says about you start saying the same thing BOLDLY AND OUT LOUD!

Eventually you will start seeing yourself as God sees you!

Stay with it until you do!

Fifty-Four

You Can Have What You Say (Part 3)

We will continue our lessons on this subject from the past two months coming from a little different angle so as to make it clear. As you study these lessons it would do you well to determine to act upon these instructions. You see it is knowledge acted upon that brings results!

We can say we believe the Bible, but until we act on the scripture it will be only a mental assent, or head knowledge". Or maybe I should put it this way.

Faith Is An Act

Faith is an act. We try to believe the Word and figure it out with our minds, when all that is necessary is to act on the word in some way! Do what it says! Move something you could not move before! Your arm, leg, etc. Or you could start shouting the victory! Or praising the Lord for the answer before the answer manifests!

DO SOMETHING!

Act as though God's Word were true!

James 1:22
But, be ye doers of the word, and not hearers only, deceiving your own selves.

Now to the new aspect of "You Can Have What You Say"!

Romans 4:17-21
17 (As it is written, I have made thee a father of many nations,) before him whom he believed, even God, who quickeneth (makes alive) the dead, and calleth those things which be not as though they were.
18 Who against hope believed in hope, that he might become the father of many nations, according to that which was spoken, So shall thy seed be.
19 And being not weak in faith, he considered not his own body now dead, when he was about an hundred years old, neither yet the deadness of Sarah's womb:
20 He staggered not at the promise of God through unbelief; but was strong in faith, giving glory to God;
21 And being fully persuaded that, what he had promised, he was able also to perform.

Here we find God speaking to Abraham, and foretelling his future! God tells Abraham that he is soon to be a father of many nations, when he was nearly a hundred years old!

He is calling those things that be not as though they were!

Speaking of things that do not exist (in the natural realm) as though they did! Hallelujah! Do you see it? God is speaking what He desires into existence! But! In this case Abraham must believe it before it will come to pass because he is involved! Or, Abraham must act upon the promise before it will come to pass!

PAST TENSE

Notice how God makes this statement! ***"I have made you the father of many nations!"***

This statement was made as a statement of fact (Past tense!) before Abraham had any children!

Well, you might say, He is God"!

Well consider this! Up until that time Abraham's name was Abram. God changed his name to Abraham (Father of multitudes)

And Abraham received the new name. He started calling himself Abraham" setting himself in agreement with God! He did not even consider his old aged body, neither did he consider Sarah's barren womb! He was fully persuaded that God was able to do what He said! He even started giving God Glory for the child before he was even born!

I can just see Abraham walking around his compound saying very boldly "Sarah and I are going to have a baby!" People would looked at him as if he had lost his mind! NO! He is calling those things which be not as though they were like his God!

Yep! One would probably say to another in a whisper! It must be Alzheimers!

But Abraham was not looking at the natural things! He did not even consider them of any consequence! God had spoken and that was enough for him!

Real faith has nothing to do with anything except God's Word!

> *Romans 10:17*
> *So then faith cometh by hearing, and hearing by the word of God.*

The word translated *hearing* here in every other place means obedience".

Hence we could say it like this faith comes by hearing the word with the intent to do it"!

It seems we rarely see this kind of faith any more! When the church finds out what real faith is, we will have that mighty revival everyone is talking about!

So how are we to act on this lesson we have learned from God's Word?

Set yourself in agreement with God's Word! How?

If God says, and He does in *Matthew 8:17,* that Jesus took our infirmities, and bare our sicknesses then you add your amen to that and say the same thing! (This statement of fact was made to you, just as God made His promise to Abraham before Isaac was born) Even if you are being attacked with illness be like Abraham and do not consider your own body, but consider the promises of God!

Start calling yourself healed! (Abraham started calling himself what God said! Why can't you?) Well! Blessed! Strong! Rich! Happy!

Start calling your kids, husband, wife, and all your family saved!

No matter what the problem, agree with God! After all He is smarter than you! (Isn't He?) And if He says you are healed, just swallow real big and say? Yes I am according to the Word of God! Then hold fast your confession!

> *Hebrews 10:23*
> *Let us hold fast the profession of our faith without wavering; (for he is faithful that promised;)*

Dare to call those things that be not as though they were until they come into existence! Don't just try it!

Just Do It!!

Is God's Word the FINAL AUTHORITY in your life? It can be, it should be.

"Rick serves up a full meal of God's Word, teaching Heaven's truths and testifying of those truths operating for him and others right here on the earth. 'Matthew 4:4' is a FAITH BUILDER from cover to cover." - *Aaron Jones*
Author and Minister
Tulsa, Oklahoma

Available at select Bookstores and

www.boldtruthpublishing.com

www.ingramcontent.com/pod-product-compliance
Lightning Source LLC
La Vergne TN
LVHW051458080426
835509LV00017B/1809

9780998153148